12/13

BRAINTREE
LIBRARY

2 2 FEB 2014

2015

1 5 AUG 2016

BTR

D0230230

30130503047690

EVERYMAN'S
ENGLAND

Victor Canning (1911–1986) is best known as a thriller writer, though he also wrote historical romances and books for children. Over a writing career spanning 50 years, he wrote more than 60 books and over 80 short stories. Many of his books have been filmed.

Charles Collingwood is a British actor renowned for his role as Brian Aldridge in the BBC Radio 4 soap opera *The Archers*. He is the author of *Brian and Me: Life on – and off – The Archers*.

EVERYMAN'S ENGLAND

Victor Canning

summersdale

EVERYMAN'S ENGLAND

This edition published in 2011 by Summersdale Publishers Ltd.
First published by Hodder and Stoughton Ltd in 1936.

Copyright © 2011 Charles Collingwood, the Estate of Victor Canning.

All rights reserved.

No part of this book may be reproduced by any means, nor transmitted, nor translated into a machine language, without the written permission of the publishers.

The right of Victor Canning to be identified as the author of this work has been asserted by the Estate of Victor Canning in accordance with sections 77 and 78 of the Copyright, Designs and Patents Act 1988.

Condition of Sale
This book is sold subject to the condition that it shall not, by way of trade or otherwise, be lent, re-sold, hired out or otherwise circulated in any form of binding or cover other than that in which it is published and without a similar condition including this condition being imposed on the subsequent publisher.

Summersdale Publishers Ltd
46 West Street
Chichester
West Sussex
PO19 1RP
UK

ESSEX COUNTY
COUNCIL LIBRARY

www.summersdale.com

Printed and bound in Great Britain by CPI Mackays, Chatham ME5 8TD

ISBN: 978-1-84953-169-6

Substantial discounts on bulk quantities of Summersdale books are available to corporations, professional associations and other organisations. For details telephone Summersdale Publishers on (+44-1243-771107), fax (+44-1243-786300) or email (nicky@summersdale.com).

CONTENTS

INTRODUCTION

In reading Victor Canning's reflective views as he journeyed from top to toe in England, what struck me was how quickly time has passed and with so much change. It is quite hard to believe he wrote *Everyman's England* within the lifetime of so many of us. The very fact that in chapter one, 'Northwood Ho!', he travels by overnight sleeper to Berwick-on-Tweed only serves to underline my point.

Throughout the book, he manages to create pictures that are enchanting yet unromantic. His style is never twee but full of surprise. His dry humour is with us all the while and his pithy, slightly leftfield opinions occasionally allow the reader to question his views as the pages fly by.

For me, it is hard not to feel that this book will remind some and inform others of a gentler, slower age while at the same time making it impossible to ignore the poverty and the hardships many had to endure not so long ago, whether within the industrial heartlands or out in the remotest, bleakest parts of our countryside. It shows the speed in which our nation's industrial decline has taken place. How fortunate we are today though that many of yesteryear's physical hardships are behind us.

I knew Victor well. He was, in later life, my father Jack's best friend and fiercest golf opponent. In his sixties, through my parents, he met and married my godmother Adria. Quite simply, for the next ten years, he was the love of her life and when he died most of the joy of life left her too. All that remained were her memories and his wonderful books.

That's what we all have with *Everyman's England*, his memories of England. Slip back a few years and spend some time in the company of a true, English gentleman.

Oh, and finally, Victor was quite insistent that this isn't a guidebook. He's right, but it would still serve as an invaluable companion to one.

Charles Collingwood, 1 April 2011

PREFACE

What does the word England mean to you? Do you think, at once, of a small patch of red tucked away at the top right-hand corner of the North Atlantic Ocean on a Mercator's projection, or of Westminster Bridge flattened by the bulk of Big Ben? Or do you think of white figures on a cricket field, *The Times*, a crowd cheering some royal pageant... To all of us England means something different, and yet I think there is for every man and woman some little corner which is more England than anywhere else. I think of a village on the River Tamar, a bridge over a Somerset stream, and the quiet of a small town near the East Coast. You may think of Brighton and the Pilgrims' Way, or the factory-studded splendour of the Great West Road and the White Stone pond on Hampstead Heath of a May morning.

Yet, if we each have our own idea of what England means, we show a lively curiosity in the England of other people, in those towns and counties which differ from our own by the accident of history and industry, and when we have the chance we visit them. Divorced from the parochialisms of familiar surroundings, held by few ties, and governed by our curiosity, we are impressed by a rich sense of our own individuality as we walk in strange places and watch the ways of other men and women. Without these occasional pilgrimages to the other man's England it would be impossible to understand the intricate pattern and appreciate the colour of the great fabric of English life.

With this thought I have written this book of the impressions I have gathered by visiting, and living in, various parts of England, in the hope that on reading these pages you may find old memories awakening in you, or feel the desire to make the same discoveries yourself. They are not all well-known places, for the simple reason that the England we treasure, each in our heart, seldom is famous, and sometimes has no claim to the beauty that guidebooks love to extol in tired adjectives, and in those places which draw thousands of tourists I am afraid I did not always pay my respects to the curiosities which have given them fame. For this unpardonable evasion I offer no excuse other than the reminder that this is not a guidebook.

Crundale

V. C.

CHAPTER 1

NORTHWARD HO!

I travelled from King's Cross to Berwick-on-Tweed in a sleeper on the night-express for no other reason than that I like to read in bed and, at the same time, feel that I am being rushed forward at a tremendous speed. To have your shoes cleaned and your hair trimmed while you read the paper is, somehow, to have scored off life. Minutes, valuable minutes, have been saved by this multiplicity of attention. Just why you should bother to save minutes hardly affects the joy of saving them. To read or sleep while a train rushes you through the night gives the same joy. To anyone who doubts that man is indeed a noble, capable creature, more than ready to conquer the irritating exigencies of life, and a being far removed from the rest of the animal world, I would recommend a journey in a sleeper.

The compartment itself is a compact of all that man holds most dear. The bed (though it does not provide for those who roll in their sleep) is comfortable, and there is generally a spare blanket on the rack above the bed if you feel you must have four blankets. Into one wall of the compartment is fitted an elaborate chromium-plated device which, after various knobs and levers have been pulled out and cursed, shows itself to be a wash-basin, fitted with hot and cold water taps. If you run too much water into the basin, it gracefully overflows on to your pyjama trousers from the jolting of the train. When you have washed, if you wish to write a letter, the basin will obligingly convert itself into a table without pinching your fingers more than three times. Hung about the compartment are enough hooks and racks to shame the untidiest of men into hanging up his clothes instead of dropping them on to the floor. That the clothes sometimes drop off in the night can be no fault of the hooks, but is due to the movement of the train and the carelessness with which they have been hung, or so I like to think.

But the greatest joy is the array of switches over the head of the bed. A man has an excuse for not sleeping if he is tempted into operating them all. Such is our delight in mechanical contraptions that there are few of us today who can resist the digital appeal of switches. One switch puts on a light over the wash-basin, another brings on a bluish reading light from a bulb over the bed, and yet another operates the general compartment light. When you have finished playing with the lights, you can begin to experiment with the levers which control the heat – three positions – and those which affect the conditioning of the air. When light, heat and air have been arranged to produce a satisfactory effect of comfort and well-being, there is still the little bell-push for the attendant.

You summon him, just to see if the bell does work, and then when he comes you have to order morning tea because you have not enough assurity of manner to say calmly that you were merely experimenting with the bell-push. And you hate tea in bed.

By this time you are wide awake, and you are no longer interested in the book, so you decide to lie awake in the dark, watching the lights from small towns and the windows of country houses as they swirl like meteors across the little heaven of the carriage window. Beneath you the bed sways gently and the wheels beat out a tantalising, never-changing rhythm. You finally go to sleep wishing that you had travelled by day, for then you need not have watched lights stream across the dark rectangle of the window, but could have sat watching ever-changing scenery, or have been diverted by the man opposite who turns out to be a traveller in farm tractors and not, as you had hoped, a vaudeville actor on the way to another date.

My train brought me into Berwick, in the early sunshine of a morning which had somehow strayed from June into March, over the lofty, straddling viaduct designed by Robert Stephenson. There are three bridges over the Tweed at Berwick, dwindling in size like the three bears: the large railway bridge, then the new Border Bridge, its whiteness making the others look rather shabby, and the Tweed Bridge, the smallest of the three, but by far the oldest.

From the carriage window I had a view of the wide, grey-green Tweed rolling in spate to the sea. The right bank of the river was flat and cut into meadows, brightened by the fresh colours of new houses, while the other bank rose sharply to an eminence, darkened upstream by patches of trees and gorse that still showed yellow points of bloom. Downstream, below the bridge, the hill was covered by the houses and streets of Berwick.

Berwick has a medieval air; its red roofs, the thin twists of smoke curling up from hidden chimneys, and the friendly clustering and pushing of the houses up the steep slope reminded me of illustrations of Hans Andersen's fairy stories. I would not swear that the chimneys are crooked or that there are quaint turrets poking through the smoke, though I felt that the chimneys and roofs knew all about Hans Andersen and that it was only a regard for the convenience of the inhabitants which kept them from a crooked way of life.

The town has that somnolent air of a border town whose inhabitants have long forgotten the need for armed vigilance, for the men and women who walk in the streets are the descendants of folk who used to spend the best part of their lives fighting to preserve their independence and livelihoods. For centuries Berwick was an excuse for fighting between the English and the Scots; first one had it and then the other, and between 1147 and 1482 it changed hands as many as thirteen times. It has a record for sieges which almost equals that of Jerusalem, and probably no other town in England has seen as much fighting. But Berwick, especially in the thirteenth century, was worth fighting for; its Customs receipts then were reckoned to account for almost a quarter of the whole sum collected in England. The only tangible trace of its stormy history today rests in the old walls which are in a state of preservation that rivals those of York and Chester. The walls are mostly Elizabethan, though there are the remains of an earlier Edwardian fortification.

This information about Berwick's walls I have, obviously, obtained from a guidebook. Alone, I am quite incapable of differentiating between an Elizabethan, Edwardian, or back wall. Exactly in the reign of which of the Edwards, who preceded Elizabeth, the earlier wall was built, my guidebook (and various others I consulted) did not say, and I am not well enough versed in the Scottish and English pre-Elizabethan Edwards to decide. If the mystery worries any reader I can only refer him to the British Museum.

It is a long time since soldiers manned the bastions and sentinelled the ramparts, and where pikemen thrust down at the invaders, the children of the town now play ball, and the old men walk quietly in the sun exercising their dogs. As I got out of the train and stood on the railway platform it was hard to imagine that where the steel rails now run and porters shout to one another, once stood the great Berwick Castle, and that on one of its towers, in 1306, the Countess of Buchan was shut up in a wooden cage to spend six years exposed to the public gaze to expiate the sin of exercising her prerogative, as a daughter of the house of Fife, of crowning the Scottish kings. She had, with a hastily improvised crown, made Robert Bruce King of Scotland at Scone. Six years in a wooden cage would make a man morose. With a woman it would probably produce a very bad temper, and I can imagine that if there was any shouting of taunts at the good lady she probably gave as good as she got.

When you go to Berwick you must walk down Station Street, close by the station, and look at the house on the right corner at the top of the street. It is a large, square, grey house, and as I came abreast of it a pigeon flew over it with a clapping of wings which made me look up and see what otherwise would have been easy to miss. A stone coping ran along the top of the house and at each corner and, so it seemed to me, wherever there was space for one, stood a bust of a man. For a moment I stared at this decorated roof-top and then through the clear morning air I was aware that the faces which looked down upon me were vaguely familiar. I stared hard and then, despite the weathering they had undergone, I was sure that I was looking at Robbie Burns and Sir Walter Scott and other well-known figures. There they all were perched up on the roof-top. Dickens, Byron, the Duke of Wellington... basking in the sunlight and enjoying the view.

How did they get there, and why? Did the builder of the house have an opportunity to buy a job lot of busts and use them to decorate his house? For a moment I was determined to knock at the house door and discover the reason, and then I hesitated. It was just breakfast time and I knew what kind of a reception I might get from a busy housewife if I interrupted the cooking of porridge and ham and eggs with questions of busts and Robbie Burns. I wish now that I had not faltered for my curiosity is growing every day and sometimes threatens to keep me awake at night. I know that someday I shall be dragged back to Berwick for the single purpose of satisfying my curiosity.

I met an old man lounging over the parapet of Berwick's newest bridge. He was one of those men who look so old that it is difficult to imagine that they were ever boys, and who have, you feel, a grand scorn of anything which is young. His clothes had that drab colour and indeterminate look which indicate, but are no longer affected by, the passage of time, and he was shouting down emphatic but unintelligent remarks to a youth who was painting a rowing boat on a landing stage below the bridge. The youth ignored him completely, not I felt from any disrespect for his age, but because he did not suspect that he was being addressed. A stiff wind was blowing out to sea and shredding the old man's words into silence. Seeing me the old man stopped his shouting and spat into the gutter. I took this as a mark of friendliness and, seeking to raise his civic pride and ingratiate myself in his good favour, I remarked on the beauty of Berwick's bridges.

'They're troublesome in the summer,' he replied.

'In the summer?' I wondered what mystery there was about them which made them troublesome in the summer.

'Not for an old skin like mine,' he went on happily. 'Midges like young blood.'

'Bridges,' I boomed, 'not midges.'

He shook his head and eyed the youth painting the boat. I saw that I was losing his attention, so I asked him loudly whether, despite the official inclusion of Berwick as an English town, he considered himself Scottish or English.

'Wha's that?' he asked, screwing up one side of his face.

I repeated my question, shouting almost.

He shook his head sorrowfully. 'I'm awfa' dull o' hearin',' he confessed.

So I came closer to him, determined to bring some coherence into the conversation, and bawled my question until I could have been heard at Spittal on the other side of the Tweed. He laughed and scratched the stubble on his chin.

17

'We're neither,' he said, 'we're Berwickers!'

And Berwickers they are; Border people who, until recent years, never knew whether they belonged to England or Scotland, for the town used to change hands with a frequency that, despite its dangers, must have become monotonous for the citizens, and between 1551 and 1885 it was a neutral town belonging to no country – a town, county and country all on its own so that Great Britain was England, Ireland, Scotland, Wales, and Berwick-on-Tweed. Now it is part of Northumberland, but the men and women are 'Berwickers' still.

With the sunlight on it Berwick is a wealth of red, grey and gold. The red pantiles of the old houses flash in the warm sun, and the grey lengths of the grass-topped ramparts and bastions, relics of its fortified days, which surround the town, take on a dignity and beauty which make one forget their ugly, medieval purpose. Everywhere there is a continual air of friendliness and kind curiosity. In larger towns the stranger passes unnoticed; in Berwick there is time and space to mark him for attention. As I walked down Hatter's Lane, a typical Berwick street of red-roofed houses, holed by dark doorways that lead back to dim courtyards, a man approached a group of shawled women and enquired by name for someone living in the street.

He was accorded no perfunctory directions. The women with common assent formed themselves into a bodyguard and escorted him, volubly, up the street to the house. Here, one obligingly opened the door and called to Mrs So-and-so, meanwhile the others grouped themselves about him, and perhaps fearing that he might want to shirk the interview at the last moment, assured him that this was where Mrs So-and-so lived. It was not until he had made his preliminaries with Mrs So-and-so and had been invited into the front parlour that the other women withdrew, their faces happy at the accomplishment of their obvious duty towards a stranger.

I spent a morning walking about the streets and gradually the placid, contented atmosphere of the town began to steal about me until I felt that there was no world outside of this grey and red town over the river, that all the haste and turmoil of the world, the madness of internecine quarrel and wordy pact-making had no significance, and that the main purpose of mankind was to lean against a shop doorway, uncaring whether customers came, talking to the man across the way and occasionally bidding Mrs Sinclair or Mrs Jarvis good morning, or better still, if one ached for action, to lead a dog along the grass-topped ramparts and feel the sea breeze upon one's face and smell the salt in the air... Even the Great North Road which crosses the new bridge seems to lose its hurry and bustle through the town, as though the drivers sense the gentle spirit of calm that drenches everything and unconsciously slacken their pace below even the statutory thirty miles an hour.

Only by the quayside and out by the harbour mouth is that feeling of inactivity dissipated. It is here that the real life of Berwick pulsates, for the Berwickers are fishermen, who draw into their nets not ordinary fish, but that king of fish, the salmon.

'Such a fish! shining silver from head to tail, and here and there a crimson dot; with a grand hooked nose and grand curling lip, and a grand bright eye, looking round him proudly as a king, and surveying the water right and left as if all belonged to him. Surely he must be the salmon, the king of all fish.'

It is easy to picture the awe of lonely Tom at his first sight of a salmon. Even in death there is something about salmon which commands man's respect, to see him in his proper element as Tom did, and mark the lordly glance of that patrician eye was more than enough to make a water-baby suddenly tremble.

In Berwick, from February until September, the salmon is truly king. For the whole of the thirty weeks of the season salmon are caught, talked of, dreamt about, and sometimes eaten by the blue-jerseyed, sea-booted fishermen.

Whenever the tide permits, and they can only work at certain states of the tide, groups of fishermen may be seen at their stations along the river, from the mouth of the Tweed where it swirls out across the bar to the North Sea, to well above the great railway viaduct.

I walked at low tide out across the wet sands and patches of bladder wrack to where one crew was stationed just inside the harbour mouth. There were six men working their wear-net. The method of fishing is very simple. One end of the net is fastened by a rope to a portable windlass on the shore, the net is folded neatly into the stern of the boat and this is rowed upstream until it is far enough from the bank to shoot the net. The boat turns downstream in a circle, the net slipping over the stern as it goes. When the boat comes into the bank the rope on the other end of the net is fastened to another wind-lass and then commences the work of hauling, so often a disappointing task.

Three times I watched this particular crew shoot their net and each time there was nothing in it except a few dead branches and clumps of sea grass. Once, as they were folding the net back into the boat for another shot, a rent was discovered in the mesh. From the pocket of an old man with a greying beard came a wooden needle and thread and the net was repaired as they stood, ankle-deep, in the water. A cold wind blew in from the sea, fretting at their jerseys, and from the sands across the river came the crying of sea-birds, but the men seemed oblivious of everything except the net in their hands. They spoke very little to each other as the old man picked up the meshes and worked his needle in and out with a dexterity that was worthy of a woman. To them, though they would never express themselves so, the nets were sacred and their reverence was evidenced in the care with which they handled them...

At the next shot they were lucky, and three salmon came flapping and jerking to the sands. The greybeard carried them up the beach in a pannier and we began to talk.

The fishing stations, he told me, are now owned by fishing companies who pay the crews a regular weekly wage and a percentage on their season's catch; though at one time the stations belonged to individuals and some of them had been in the hands of the same family for generations.

'It's a grand business,' the old fisherman confessed in a moment of enthusiasm, and then added with characteristic caution: 'but ye ken it has its disappointments.' I thought of the times I had seen the nets shot without results and agreed with him.

He put the pannier down and pointed out the fish to me: 'That's a grilse,' he said, indicating one of them, a handsome silvery fish that even in death retained a graceful strength and beauty; 'a fish that is coming up from the sea for the first time since leaving the river where it was spawned.'

A salmon is generally called anything but a salmon, and the profusion of its different names points the various phases in its life. As the eel must leave pond and stream to journey down river and across the ocean to spawn in the dark fathoms of the far Sargasso, so the salmon must leave the sea and journey up river to the gravelly reaches of moorland becks and streams to spawn.

After hatching in the river the young fry grow into parr, and at the end of two years in the river the sea claims them.

Drawn downstream and out over the bar they become smolt. In the sea the fish develops its true salmon colours, and on its first return to the river becomes a grilse. The salmon stay in the sea for a varying number of years, and while they are there they reach full sexual maturity. After passing up the river and spawning they are known as kelts, emaciated, haggard fish that drift apathetically back to the sea there to recover their colour and vitality. For all the able research which has been done there is still much of the salmon's life which is a mystery. What deep-seated instinct keeps it moving from sea to river? It has been suggested that, as swallows migrate from the coming winter to the burgeoning summer of a far country, so salmon migrate from the rivers of decreasing oxygen content to the sea and a higher oxygen content, obeying some chemical impulse in their bodies which is prompted by lessening or increasing oxygen in the water. The theory is a plausible and ingenious one, but fish are not so easily observed as birds and the mystery of the salmon's movements may be with us for a long time yet.

It was darkening as I left the town and the bulky shape of the hill was speckled with growing lights. As the train crossed the viaduct I caught the gleam of a lantern down-river, and I guessed that the fishermen were hard at work, for when the tide forces them to it, they must work during the night. I knew that the old grey beard would be at his station, tugging at the oars or straining at the handle of a windlass to draw from the water that harvest of mystery and beauty which, even when it is served to us from a can, still retains a royal flavour; a flavour acquired during those dark, secret years in the sea when salmon harried herring and nosed around weed-strewn rocks unknown to man.

CHAPTER 2

CUMBERLAND CONTRASTS

The coastal road between the two Cumberland towns of Silloth and Maryport is about thirteen miles long. They are thirteen such miles as may change a man's mood from pessimism to optimism, and startle him from happiness to sadness within a hundred paces.

Silloth in name has a biblical sound. Poetically David and Samuel might have fled from Saul to Silloth in Ramah and the verse would have sounded as well.

'Behold, David is at Naioth in Ramah' – And behold I was at Silloth in Cumberland on a cold winter's day, and the imagery of romantic speculation which I had built around the town's name fell from me. I should have known better than to have relied upon a name.

As a town Silloth presents to the casual visitor more works of man than of grace, and the works of man are not inspiring. The moment I entered it I felt depressed and spiritless. Perhaps the fault lay in my stars and not in the town. There are people, I have no doubt, who are prepared to swear by Silloth and praise its esoteric charms before all.

The tall stack of a busy flour mill, the bulging horror of a gasometer and the painted funnel of a cargo boat in the harbour, and everywhere that lifeless feeling of four o'clock in the afternoon – that is how I remember Silloth. Few people walked the streets, its hotels and shops looked dead and a cold wind sweeping in from the Solway Firth kept the papers dancing in the gutters and drove me away from the sea-front. I decided to leave Silloth and walk to Maryport. If I have wronged Silloth I apologise, but rather would I have wronged it than have chanced spending a night in the town...

From Silloth the road runs, twisting very little, along the great sweep of coast to Maryport. Here and there it cuts through the folds of the land that reach down to the sea, forming tiny bluffs that sometimes shelter bungalows and domesticated railway carriages and omnibus bodies. The ubiquity of the railway carriage is a characteristic of these times. It has always been a great mystery to me how these heavy compartments have reached some of the places which I have seen them gracing. Yes, gracing, for some have been so tricked out with bright paint and bedecked with brighter flowers, set about with well-kept gardens and crowned by crooked chimney pots that they have a gnomish air of concealing a host of delights. At one time if a man wished to eschew the transient and wicked pleasures of the world and give his life to the contemplation of his navel and lofty thoughts, he bought himself a hair shirt (I have always thought that this item must have been remarkably short to allow the practice of his first exercise) and retired to some isolated cave in the midst of a wilderness, from whence he would emerge at intervals to place lost travellers on the right road for Bath-Sheba, Ilion or Alexandria, or, if there was bad weather about entertain them in his cave for the evening on goat's milk, dates and the fantastic story of his youth, until the storm had passed. Today, if a man has a craving for solitude, he buys himself some of the Great Western Railway Company's discarded rolling stock and, by some method of which I am not aware, gets his railway carriage taken to the edge of the Cumberland fells, and there spends the rest of his life cultivating his polyanthus and godetia, smoking a pipe and sometimes chatting over the fence with the A.A. man in a way which has no sign of the rancour which might be expected from the A.A. man's usurpation of his ancient privileges towards lost travellers. Some of these modern hermits still keep goats, but the hair shirt has gone out of fashion.

When I left Silloth bright sunshine was filling the Firth with blue, leaping shadows, and tiny catspaws chased one another over the water. In the distance was the hazy outline of the Isle of Man, and I knew from the piling cloud masses that before I reached Maryport I might find myself encompassed by a snowstorm and discover the dark shape of Skiddaw inland hidden by a grey canopy. To my left were fields, brown patches of wasteland and the marshes, or mosses as the natives call them. Behind the fields, hedged about by stone walls, and across the long stretches of marsh, rose the faint outline of the Lakeland fells. I thought of Wastwater and brooding Scafell, and I remembered a hot day in the May of King George's Jubilee year. There was to be a Jubilee bonfire on top of Scafell and for weeks before the day there were piles of wood in Wastdale, Borrowdale and other convenient places, with little notices requesting walkers who were going to climb Scafell to take at least one piece of timber with them to the bonfire. The request sounds simple. Actually it is a work of no little honour and devotion to climb Scafell, hugging to your breast a young tree. Although the path is clear and not difficult, it is long and exhausting, and before the peak is reached a man is glad to have his hands free and sometimes wishes he could rid himself of the weight of the sandwiches in his pocket.

I started out to climb Scafell from the Langdale side, by way of Rossett Gill and Angle Tarn. A pile of wood in the valley made no appeal to me. I knew Scafell, and I thought, unloyally perhaps, that if King George wanted a bonfire in so inconvenient a spot other people must attend to it. My wan patriotism did not impair my enjoyment of the scramble up Rossett Gill, but at Angle Tarn, lying by the dark waters, I came across a stout length of ash trunk, deserted by some fervent but short-winded wood-carrier. To have carried it so far was an achievement. I decided that it should not lie deserted by the tarnside to rot. It should be taken to the pike and there burn merrily in honour of the King's Jubilee. On a sudden I was the most patriotic man in the Lake District.

The story of the carrying of that log is an odyssey. Many times I longed to jettison it; many times I cursed the villain who had left it by the lakeside to tempt me, many times I tripped and cut myself, many times it tripped me and clouted my shins, but in the end it rested up-ended in the pile of wood securely wired to the top of the pike. Two days later I finished a late supper in a Borrowdale cottage and walked out into the balmy dusk of a May evening to watch the beacon blaze to which I had contributed. That was to be my joy, my reward, to know that the new star blazing in the sable heaven owed some of its light to my toil, that I had laboured to help create that burst of orange and gold flame which was to light the rocky slopes of Scafell and signal to the other beacons which stretched across the country from end to end. I never saw the fire. It was a clear night and I stood on my vantage-point, recommended by the cottage wife, but no light suddenly sprang into life in the darkness. I waited until I was cold and I knew that the fire, if it had been lighted, must have burnt out. The next morning I found out that I had mistaken the good lady's directions and had waited in the wrong place, for between me and Scafell during my vigil had towered a host of fells and crags that hid from me even the glowing of the sky where the beacon blazed away, where my log burned to red ash and then scattered in the wind, grey flakes to be lost among the hills. I never told the cottage wife that I did not see the blaze. I have told this story many times to many people and always I have lied admirably, describing my proud sensations as I watched that flare of flame on Scafell. But now I must tell the truth, for a good lie should die soon to preserve its richness, and it deserves an honest grave.

The whole stretch of coast is a sanctuary for birds. On the firm islands of sand which lie out beyond the banks of grey shingle and stone, I saw companies of black-and-white oyster catchers, their heads to the wind, looking like a convention of waiters mysteriously isolated. Oyster catchers are very much like waiters in their habits; sometimes they stand wrapt in sombre idleness, eyeing the waste of sand with a weary expression of resignation, and at times they are spurred into a frenzy of activity, rushing here and there, prying with their long bills beneath the stones, turning over seaweed, for all the world as though they were in a City restaurant in the rush hour.

Wheeling in the breeze above the oyster catchers were clouds of gulls; the dainty black-headed gulls, their black caps at this time of the year changed for a white head-dress that hinted at its spring beauty by a black spot above the eye, the rapacious herring gulls, the swashbucklers of the sea, and here and there were those aloof Vikings, the great black-backed gulls that roam from the Arctic to the Equator with the same nonchalance that a clerk goes by tube from Belsize Park to the Bank. These last are now not so common as they were, and on the Kent and Essex coasts, where they were once common and known as cobs, they are very rare. It is the largest and, I think, the most beautiful of the British gulls, and to watch it in flight is to become conscious of the extraordinary power and dexterity of wing which these birds possess.

I have watched a cloud of gulls, perhaps some two hundred, wheeling and dipping over the carcass of a dead pig brought up by the tide while a wind at nearly gale force has been blowing, and in the midst of all their wild swooping, circling and dipping I have never seen one collision or anything which looked like an error of judgment. Man likes to pride himself upon his conquest of the air and his powers of flight. Two hundred aeroplanes mixed together like the gulls would produce a pretty carnage.

I walked for some time with the company of the gulls and other birds. The grey, wintry sky flashed with the points of their wings and the wind was alive with the noise of their screaming. Flying low along the water's edge, just skimming the waves, went curlew, redshank, uttering their thin, protesting pipe, and wild duck. The fields on the other side of the road held colonies of fieldfares and lapwings.

At Salta I came across a farmer leaning on a gate and watching a flock of black-faced Highland ewes nibbling at a feed of turnips. He laughed as I stopped in the lee of the hedge and tried to beat life back into my frozen fingers. The sky had darkened to a deep indigo and once or twice spits of snow came whistling in the wind.

'Cold?' he questioned.

I blew on my fingers and he laughed again and then spoke in the Cumberland accent which is hard at times for a southerner to follow.

'How would you like to lie out on yon moss for three hours waiting for the geese to come back at night?' he asked.

I told him that if geese-shooting entailed such endurance it was not likely to find me among its enthusiasts.

His eyes were creased at the corners with crow's-feet wrinkles and were a hard, healthy blue. He stood easily against the wind as he talked, his hands in his breeches pockets, a cap to one side of his head, and his jacket open to show an old woollen yellow waistcoat. I was almost shivering in a top-coat; he seemed oblivious of the cold and the sudden spurts of snow.

We stood looking over the marsh towards the coast, talking of the lambing season that would come in March, and he explained that the characteristic rounded thatched haystacks of the district were raised on circular stone platforms, about eighteen inches high, to prevent the rainwater that runs off the thatching from soaking into the bottom of the rick. In no other part of England which I have visited have I seen this precaution so generally adopted.

He lived in one of those grey Cumberland houses which, having no pretensions to beauty, being no more than four walls and a slate roof, somehow seem to harmonise perfectly with the countryside. When men, it seems, make use of local materials, build they never so badly, the stone carries with it the fitness which it had in its natural state and which defeats ugliness even in its new condition. The stone houses and flaked tiles of the Cotswolds, the red-bricked thatched cottages of Kent and the flint-walled houses of Hertfordshire have this beauty.

When I left the farmer it was snowing heavily. Down on the marsh some men had set fire to the dead grass and reeds to keep down the vermin that find a refuge there. Great streamers of smoke and flame flared away in the wind, twisting and coiling like angry snakes beneath the lowering sky. I stood, forgetting the cold in the beauty of the scene. A dark purple, gravid sky showed long barriers of cloud hurrying in from the sea to pile in great fantastic mounds above the fells inland. The green rock-brake on the stone walls trembled in the wind beneath the bracken skeletons, and a lapwing skirled through the air above me. The lashing tongues of flame were beaten close to the earth by the wind and fled from tip to tip of the clumps of dead grass, forming a string of tiny pyres that flared and wickered for a while and then died to a smouldering, smoky red gleam. The clouds swung lower, swathes of snow slanted earthwards, lodging in the wall crevices, and suddenly I became aware of something apocalyptic, some awful purpose in the play of natural forces, the fire, the snow, and the growl and smash of the sea mixed with the high whine of the wind. My whole being was tensed towards that awful moment when all these powers should break loose and run, maddened and uncontrollable, across the country, the fire roaring and devouring, the wind flattening and cruel, while the soft, pitiless snow followed softly behind them, covering the ruin with its uncharitable mantle. Human life was very insignificant before that display of elemental things...

All around was a wild, barren beauty, a rude beauty which grew upon me, wooing by direct assault and battering me into admiration, until I was aware only of the crying of the sea-birds, the thunder of the breakers flinging their white crests over the cobble-drafts, and the tossing of the thin spikes of dune grass before the oncoming flames.

Allonby is no more than a handful of houses, halfway between the two towns. A small stream runs by the side of the road through the village, and as I entered a little old lady was standing on a trestle bridge that crosses the stream, her shawl pulled about her against the wind, while she fed a pair of swans with bread from her basket.

It may well be that her grandmother was feeding the ancestors of those same swans on that day when Charles Dickens and Wilkie Collins came to Allonby. They stayed at the old Ship Inn during their northern tour, described in Christmas Stories. They had been in the rugged John Peel country of Caldbeck, climbing Carrock Fell, when, a mist descending upon them, Collins slipped on a wet boulder and sprained his ankle. After describing other adventures Dickens tells of their reception at Allonby:

> "Allonby, gentlemen," said the most comfortable of landladies, as she opened one door of the carriage.
> "Allonby, gentlemen," said the most attentive of landlords, as he opened the other.

I did not arrive in the style of Dickens and his companion. I was cold and longing for a hot drink and my coat was wet with melted snow. I pushed upon the door of the inn and found myself in a cold passage-way. After a few shouts the landlord appeared from somewhere in the back of the house and I was shown into a room hung with coloured prints of game birds where a coal fire burned cheerfully.

Attentiveness must be a trait of Allonby landlords, for very soon I was warm before the fire, my coat was drying over the back of a chair and I was drinking scalding hot cups of tea and attacking a plate of new bread and butter, while the landlord entertained me with an account of his life as a collier in a mine near Whitehaven.

Maryport in Dickens's day was a thriving town full of contented people. If he could visit it today, it would probably evoke from him the one literary vice of which he has been accused, an occasional tearful sentiment; sentiment – 'that odious onion,' as Birrell called it. Maryport today would call forth tears from any man, were he not conscious of the impotency of tears to remedy such state as Maryport has fallen to.

In the midst of all the wild splendour of this coast, Maryport is a tragedy. The town is built on and around a hill which overlooks the sea. From the top of the hill you can look down upon the houses which cluster around the dock-side, their grey slates marked by gulls. The streets are narrow and steep, and in places there are zigzagging steps that climb the hillside. It is a larger, darker, unhappier Clovelly of the North. In the harbour fishing boats tilt on the mud at low tide, and at night the white column of the small light at the end of the breakwater shines like a dim candle.

About the whole town is an air of dejection, as though it were brooding over past glories, and it may well be so, for once Maryport was alive and active. There were pits that employed hundreds of men, rolling mills, shipbuilding yards where some of the finest ships in the world had their birth beside the brawling River Ellen, and a constant traffic of cargo boats into the harbour to keep the dockers busy.

Now, all that has gone. The lifeblood has been drained from Maryport by forces beyond the control of the townspeople. Almost all the pits are closed, the yards have not known the ring of hammered rivets for years, the rolling mills are silent, and few cargo boats come into the harbour.

On the corners I saw groups of patient men with time on their hands, hours in which to brood over their misfortunes, and up and down the streets the tight-lipped women hurried about their shopping. The poverty of a town may well be determined by its shops. There are no luxury shops in Maryport. The atmosphere of the town was distressing, though it could not dull the laughter of the children in the streets as they played. There was a happy clatter of clogs where small boys raced up and down the stone steps.

By the harbourside things are more cheerful. There is still the fishing, though that is not so profitable as it used to be. On the tide the boats go out beyond the harbour light to find the herring and the cod, and in the inns the rough seamen jostle one another, talking of fish and boats, of nets and tides and prices. Unshaven, some of them, their caps and jerseys silvered with the loose scales of fish, they play their favourite game of dominoes and drink their beer happily enough, but they are not unaware of the tragedy of the rest of their townsmen. No man could live in Maryport and ignore it. Silloth may not be so large or picturesque as Maryport, yet it must be happier.

Whenever I think of that coast, of the seabirds and the wild sweeps of sand and shingle, of the grey houses and the sheep with their fleeces tossed by the wind, and the farmers who do not seem to feel the cold, I shall remember the men I saw along the beach as I came into Maryport. Stretching away until they were lost in the snow haze, they were bent to the shingle, like gleaners across an immense field. In their bended forms was a suggestion of grimness and evil.

My curiosity aroused, I walked over to one of them to see what he was doing. I soon learned. The men were foraging the beach for the small pieces of coal cast up by the tide from some underwater reef. The pieces of coal were hardly bigger than large peas, and stooping to the beach these men were picking the black lumps from the litter of shells and pebbles and painfully filling their sacks. A morning's work might half fill a sack, I was told by the man I spoke to, and then it had to be carried, sometimes as much as five miles, to keep the fires going in homes where fires were luxuries hard to come by. I was cold enough walking along the beach in the wind. It was only too easy to imagine what the cold would be to those men, thinly clad, and moving slowly over the pebble ridges.

Talking to this man, I was, and not for the first time, suddenly ashamed of myself and the age I lived in. He told me some details of his life and his struggle to keep his wife and children sufficiently nourished upon his relief money, and he spoke of the possibility of gaining employment in the wry, cynical manner of a man who has had most of his hope taken from him by ten years of enforced idleness and poverty. I expected him to be bitter, but instead of bitterness was resignation and apathy.

'I was bitter at first,' he confessed. 'Who wouldn't be? But it's no good to get like that. It doesn't do you any good and it only worries your family. For myself I wouldn't mind what happened. It's having a family and watching them do without things that—' He broke off and stared out across the sea. I left him, trying not to think of his thin body shivering in a wretched suit, a scraggy scarf his only extra protection against the wind…

A coast of birds, of beauty and courageous fishermen, and a coast of ghastly paradox, where men grabble in the shingle for small coals, while about Maryport stand the gaunt frames of silent pitheads that guard enough coal to fill those sacks a million times... If ever men and women had cause to despair, those men and women of Maryport and the peoples of towns that share a like fate have cause; and if ever men begin to pride themselves upon their efficiency and high civilisation let them think of the peoples of such stricken towns and be ashamed.

CHAPTER 3

TOWN OF SURPRISES

Of the Yorkshire industrial towns which I know, I like Halifax best of all. Most Yorkshire towns of the industrial area assault you with their ugliness and befuddle you with miles of tortuous tram-lined roads, flanked by pitheads and mounds of slag.

That the towns are shapeless and unplanned is a fault they share with hundreds of others. That they overflow into one another so that a stranger hardly knows when he is in Bradford or Leeds, or Wakefield or Dewsbury, and after a time begins not to care, is a fault which it is impossible to forgive and hard to bear with.

Halifax is different. It possesses everything which makes other towns ugly and yet it is beautiful. Gasometers, which would offend the eye anywhere else, in Halifax are part of a picture which is essentially titanic and grim.

As I stood on the road that runs steeply down from Beacon Hill to the valley, there was no mistaking where the town began and ended. It lies in the deep valley of the Hebble with the dark peaks of the Pennines around it, shutting it away from the rest of the world. The hills sweep around the town in almost a full circle and, in the valley-bottom and running partly up the hill-slopes in terraces, is Halifax.

It was some time before I could find the River Hebble. Standing on the iron bridge, which carries the road over the railway in the valley, I first heard and then saw the river. There it was, hemmed in by the bulk of brewery, carpet factory, railway station and goods yards, rushing and foaming along an artificial bed, bravely pretending to be a moorland stream. There is little hope for a small stream like the Hebble in a growing town. Not large enough to influence the building development, as the Thames did at Oxford and the Avon at Bath, and too small to merit special attention like the Lea and the Fleet in London, it is pushed and thwarted, forced from one channel to another and sapped to provide water for factories and laundries, until finally it disappears altogether and is remembered only by old men drinking their half-pints who call to mind the days when they fell, fished and swam in it. Someday the Hebble must disappear and the sound of rushing water in Halifax will be gone and then the silence of the brooding, impressive hills will, alone of Nature, be left to contend with the shriek of siren and the steam-crested roar of the hooters.

Oxford has been called the city of dreaming spires but, unless you know your Oxford well, you will find it difficult to choose a spot where you can see those spires to their full advantage. Halifax is a town of smoking chimney stacks, rotund gasometers and melancholy church towers and steeples, and there is no need to seek a special vantage point to see them, for every road which runs down to Halifax will give you an aerial view.

I counted nearly a hundred of the stacks from Beacon Hill before I gave up in despair. There is no denying the impression of power that comes from those chimneys. Perhaps it is the bold effect of their number. Perhaps not; but for a moment I had a glimpse into the mystery of Mammon worship. It was easy to see how firmly a man could come to believe in and reverence his own powers. Those chimneys were the smoking candles about the altar of a devilish god, a god who still remembered the child sacrifices that appeased its majesty not so long ago. Over the chimneys drifted tiny plumes of smoke, thinning in the wind down-valley.

Mixed with the stacks are the church steeples and, at the lowest point of the valley stands the beautiful square tower of the parish church, not at all out of keeping with the industrialism that surrounds it, for the Church has always been a great ally of industry, in many places preparing the ground for its advance.

The buildings of the town are constructed from the dark brown local stone. The back-ground of hills to the rows of streets and the thrusting chimneys give a feeling of immensity. Halifax is the embodiment of industry, holding all its melancholy power and strange, compelling beauty.

Halifax, I found, was a town of surprises. My first view of it coming down the hill gave me a pleasant surprise. I had expected the usual monotony of an industrial centre, and the same sordid litter which characterises most large woollen towns. I discovered instead a town which had wrung dignity and beauty from such things as stacks, gasometers, canals and mills, and, if the stone of the houses was smoke-blackened the windows and doorsteps were spotless as though every wife was house-proud.

The distinction of Halifax arises, I think, from its honesty of purpose. It pretends to no more than it is and, by its frankness and because of its unique position in a deep-valley, it has achieved a definite beauty.

There were few signs of depression in the town and unemployment, I was told, was comparatively low. A Halifax man I talked to advised me, if I knew any family man who was unemployed and worrying about work for his children, to urge him to come to Halifax.

'There may be nowt for t' old man,' he said, 'but there's plenty to be found for t'lads and lassies.'

How an unemployed man was to transfer his family to Halifax he did not say, but he was emphatic about the ease with which young people could find employment. And he was probably right, though it is not in Halifax alone that it is easier for young boys and girls to find employment while the older folk must stay idle. This preference for young men and women in industry would be a good sign if it were correlated with some system for the maintenance of their elders. Most men and women are not so fond of work that they would not be glad to give up their posts at forty and devote the rest of their lives to doing the things they have always wanted to do. It may be the rearing of bantam fowls or a study of football coupons, and there are many who, like Richard Jefferies, would be happy to stuff their pockets full of seeds and roots and walk the countryside planting bare patches or barren corners. In ten years of such leisure as this England could rival the hibiscus and bougainvillea of the West Indies with its roses, canary creeper and periwinkle. I am afraid the Great North Road will not flower with altruistically planted rows of giant hollyhocks for any of us to see them!

The man I spoke to was a typical working-class Yorkshireman. He was of middle height, with enormous shoulders and hands of a size which made the cigarette he held look ridiculous. It was Saturday and he was dressed in his weekend finery: a black bowler hat, white collar and a navy-blue suit from the pocket of which protruded a folded evening paper.

Halifax, he told me, was becoming more like Birmingham every day. I said I hoped it was not. He did not hear me. Although Halifax was primarily a woollen town, making worsteds, and carpets, other industries were springing up. There were – and I had only to look around me to confirm his words – toffee factories, silk factories, machine-making shops, brickworks, toy factories, mills and a brewery. As he spoke he was emphatic, but courteous. He often swore, yet was careful to add each time: 'You'll excuse me swearin'?' which I gladly did, for he was better than any guidebook, and his oaths lost their harshness in his mouth, for I felt that without them he would be incomplete.

There was nothing about him to suggest that he had ever in his whole life moved beyond Yorkshire. His eyes were mild and his manner that of the man who loves his friends and home town too well to wander. To my surprise, as we talked on I found that I was in the company of a Marco Polo. Here was no factory worker who had never seen more than the dark Pennines and the rugged dales. His adventures, and I would vouch for his honesty, sounded the more astounding coming from him so soberly clad in his blue suit and neat bowler.

As a boy he had gone to South America to live with a much older brother. The brother, apparently a man who relied upon his wits for a living, had to leave for Mexico hurriedly and my friend, Marco, went with him. In Mexico the brother fell in love with a Mexican dancer, shot her lover and decamped with the dark-haired lady, leaving Marco Polo behind to fend for himself. The authorities, with some reluctance, looked after Marco until he felt it was time to assert his independence, which he did, three days before he was to be shipped back to his relations in England. From Mexico he wandered north and found himself at early manhood working for gold in the Klondike, where he was often hungry and more than once escaped unpleasant deaths. An Englishman out there, who had been lucky, paid for his passage home – and he spent the money on a new outfit and a trip to New York. His money gone, he worked in steel and coal as smelter and hewer in America until the call of the Old Country was too strong. Then he worked his passage over and landed at Liverpool with very little save a fund of stories and a host of experiences, enough to set up three prolific novelists for a lifetime. And he came back in time to earn his forty pounds a week in the palmy pre-war days of northern commercialism and to save enough to make his old age very comfortable. Before I spoke to him I should have said that the nearest he had ever been to Klondike was with Charlie Chaplin in *The Gold Rush*.

From Marco I learned the story of Wainhouse's Tower, which is a prominent landmark in the town. It was built, at a time when individualism in the North was an excuse for many things, by a wealthy manufacturer so that he might overlook the garden of a neighbour who had a strong objection to being overlooked. Marco seemed to find this a great joke; but I could not help feeling sorry for that long-dead, meek (I am sure he was meek and inoffensive) man who liked the privacy of his garden to sit and smoke and watch his marigolds and to feel that he was alone. I wonder what he did to annoy the manufacturer? Perhaps his son had dared to ask to marry the manufacturer's daughter and, not getting his consent, the two had eloped and he had vented his spleen by destroying the other father's solitude.

Halifax, like America today, believes in individualism (though America has tacked the adjective 'rugged' before the noun), and has always been reluctant to give up any of its ancient rights and privileges.

As recently as the seventeenth century it cherished its curious Gibbet Law, which, established primarily to protect the wool trade from thefts, gave the inhabitants the power to execute anyone, after a trial by a jury of burgesses, found guilty of the theft of more than 13d. The site of the gibbet is still preserved by the present day Gibbet Street. With men like pleasant Mr Wainhouse about, I wonder how many innocent citizens found an undeserved death on the gibbet.

A well-known guidebook, to which I referred, devoted six of eight pages on Halifax to a description of the parish church.

Interesting as the church undoubtedly is I cannot think that it deserves, in such an interesting town, so great a preponderance of attention. Guidebooks are too much given to lengthy descriptions of architectural features, and say all too little about the town and its people. When I entered the church I found it so hot and stuffy that I could only suppose that the writer of the guidebook got mazed in the dark aisles and went on making notes until he found his way out, and that he then left Halifax hurriedly.

I might have stayed in the church a little longer than I did, had it not been for the curious wooden effigy of a bedesman, holding an alms-box. It was coloured and, although not quite life-size, had such an air of reality that I felt the eyes were following me around. Perhaps he thought I was after the altar candlesticks. A bedesman was a man appointed to say prayers in return for alms. The word *bead* means a prayer, and the phrase 'telling his beads,' has nothing to do with keeping a tally of prayers with a rosary, but means 'saying his prayers.'

Most alms houses were founded for the benefit of bedesmen so that they could live in them and pray for the soul of the founder. It seems that there have always been some men too busy to say their own prayers.

The eyes of this bedesman followed me around the church. I thought the mild reproof in them arose from my disturbing his peace. I dropped sixpence in his box to appease him. His expression never changed and gradually he began to make me feel uncomfortable until I reached a point when I was ready to see ghostly things in the gloom of the nave. I came out and left him alone. As I cast a last glance at him as I went through the doorway he seemed to be smiling with satisfaction as though he were saying 'Well, that's got rid of him!'

Two things exist in Halifax which I had not seen for a long time anywhere else. The first is the familiar figure of childhood days – the lamplighter. I met him again in Halifax, making his round of the streets with his long pole and zigzagging from one side of the road to the other. I followed him for a while, taking pleasure in his movement, and from the number of greetings which he gave and received I could see that he was still as popular as ever. The lamplighter, the closing light of winter afternoons and somewhere the rattle of teacups and the smell of toasting muffins – how many men and women as children have dropped their books when the light faded and the print became a dark patch on the page, and then, moving from the fire, have stood with their faces pressed against the cold windowpane, breath frosting the glass, waiting for the lamplighter. There was a magic in such moments, as the world dozed between day and night and the figures of the street swirled in and out of a brown haze.

And the other thing? It is that abortive garment, the product of class-consciousness and the able supporter of many a comedian's gags, the dickey. In a shop in one of Halifax's main streets I saw dickies for sale – with collars attached, and I remembered at once red-nosed comedians with straw-coloured hair raising roars of laughter as their white dickey fronts came adrift from their waistcoats at awkward moments to smack them heartily across the face. And now, even on the stage, the dickey is dying the death forced upon it by those who once favoured it. I cannot imagine that there are many waiters who still wear dickeys, and as a source of comedy it seems to have outlived its day.

CHAPTER 4

BROAD ACRES

There are two Yorkshires; one the county of woollen mills, sprawling industrial towns, smoking chimneys, polluted streams and cobbled streets, and the other, the county of wide moors, of fertile valleys, pleasant seaside resorts, and broad acres of daleland where the wanderer from the crowded cities can find peace and consolation for a life of febrile toil in the loneliness of a skyline that rims the world for miles, and in the long sweeps of valley dipping to the slow ribbon of a river.

> *Forget six counties overhung with smoke,*
> *Forget the snorting steam and piston stroke,*
> *Forget the spreading of the hideous town;*
> *Think rather of the pack-horse on the down.*

That was the advice of William Morris, a man born out of his age, and it is good and easy advice to take in Yorkshire or any other county, for no town spreads so far that it is impossible to shake free from it and the greatest pall of smoke cannot live against the winds that sweep over moorland scarps.

There are some towns and counties which are only at their best during certain parts of the year. The Holland district of Lincolnshire should, I think, be seen first of all at tulip time, when the fields are a pattern of colours brighter than any carpet that ever came from Hamadan, and the Fens when the corn is ripening and the beet waves its luscious leaves in a moving sea-green panoply. Somerset is a county of autumn, when the Quantocks smoulder with the turning bracken and the royal hues of gorse and heath, and Cornwall is of high summer with tall yellow and purple mullein spikes in the hedges and the sea a blue which blazes to silver as the eye travels towards the horizon.

I am not a Yorkshireman. If anyone jingles a bridle over my grave when I am dead I shall not arise to go horse-stealing, and probably many Yorkshiremen will want to correct me when I say that I think the best time of the year to visit the Pennines and the dale country is in those cold months at the beginning of the year when only the snowdrop has dared to show its petals and the windflowers and 'the host of spring flowers still sleep deep in the earth'. But I hold to my opinion. No doubt, because it was so when I first saw the dales. First impressions not only last; they are loveliest and their freshness never fades. January is the time to wander away from the huddle of towns into the clear air and the steel-bright landscapes of the dales. It is walking weather and man's weather.

There is something in the sweep of grey crags and the brown folds of upland pastures that is intensified by frosty days and given an austerity that is lacking on the warmer, softer days of summer. The dales reserve their full charm for those who have the courage to seek them in the winter.

Nearly all the dale rivers have preserved their beauty, and escaped the encroaching ugliness and the despoliation which follow hard upon the heels of wide roads and factories. Rivers, apart from their natural function of drainage, have been chained by man to work his utilities, they give him power and cleanse his wools and do a hundred other labours for which they get no thanks and much abuse. This is inevitable, but I do think that the rivers which have brought affluence and importance to towns should be accorded some mark of respect and thanks, though these be only symbolical. Once a year the Lord Mayor of Leeds should drive in state to one of the bridges over the Aire. There should be ceremonies made and a speech of thanks read to the river, and then with his own hands the Lord Mayor should pour into the stream, from a golden chalice, a libation of rich brown ale. Afterwards, from the hand of the fairest maiden in the city, should be dropped a bouquet of flowers to adorn the bosom of the waters, to drift seawards to commemorate the pride and gratitude of the townsfolk towards the river. At the least it would give the newspapers material to enliven our breakfast tables, and the newsreel cameras pictures to fill up those few dull minutes before the chief film begins.

I doubt whether a quart of nut-brown, or a handful of roses, could compensate Father Aire for his sufferings. Yet even if the river is spoiled for most of its length, it still has some beauty, and nothing can belittle the grandeur and surprise which mark its birth at the foot of Malham Cove. An abrupt wall of limestone rock stands like a barrier at the end of the Aire valley and from its base bubbles up the young stream, freed from the dark channels and mysterious passages of the earth, to pour away into the sunlight on a new venture – a venture which soon loses its splendour as the stream grows in girth and passes Bingley and Shipley. But if the Airedale is doomed, the others remain, and of these, I think, the most beautiful are Wensleydale and Wharfedale, and it was to Wharfedale that I first came on a day not long after Christmas.

It was a day when, although the sun had a surprising warmth, there was hoar frost in the shadow of the walls and the trees, and the grass crisped beneath my feet as I walked. From the hollows under the topmost crags there came the gleam of snow. I entered Wharfedale by Bolton Abbey, a ruin around which thousands of tourists have dutifully walked, comprehending little and making gentle, insincere gestures of awe and wonder. Most guidebooks are careful to explain that the Abbey was built by one Alice de Meschines, in 1511, as a memorial to a son who was drowned in the Strid while hunting, and then carefully explain that this cannot be true, because the son's signature appears on a charter which allowed the monks of the Abbey to receive the manor of Bolton in exchange for other concessions. If the legend has been disproved, why bother about it? It would be wiser to omit the damning proof and let us enjoy the fiction. But the writers of official guidebooks are sticklers for truth, and unpractised in the art of falsehoods. And, unless you happen to be a student of architecture, I cannot imagine that you will be interested to know that you must note there is a large, plain, circular-headed recess, high up at W. of S. wall, in connection with a narrow wall passage, for which there is no apparent reason, or that there are two fragments of a limestone slab, with indents – one for garter, and three curvilinear windows N. of aisle, in the Abbey ruin.

By the time you have worked out which is W. of S. wall and have stared at the wrong thing you will probably have a headache and a crook in your neck and wish that you could hurl one of the slabs of limestone, with indents, at the head of the writer, or push him through any kind of window, French or curvilinear. That the Abbey has beauty and once had even greater beauty is undeniable, but to have to waste a fine afternoon searching for corbels and reliquaries when you could go and sit by the river and eat your sandwiches while you speculated as to how the monks lived, whether they fished from the spot where you are sitting and whether they were such a drunken lot of merry tipplers as history reputes, is an imposition which I resent. The architectural technicalities are useful. There should also be some information for the ignorant, unenlightened being like myself who is aware that the monks who inhabited these places were alive and that the masons who carved the gargoyles and capitals were probably as cheerful and fond of their joke as the masons who walk any modern scaffolding.

I stood on the spur which overlooks the river just above the Abbey. Below me the river swirled over its boulder-strewn bed, dark and deep on the outside of the curve and frothed with rapids where it broke away over the shallows by the far bank.

All around was the silence of the fells, their bottom slopes cut into fields and the crests broken in places by black patches of firs. Farther up the valley the ridge of the hills stretched in an unbroken line against the pale grey sky with moving puffs of cloud above them. Between the black trunks of the trees I could see the weathered skeleton of the Abbey, surrounded by its green walks and lichened gravestones. The autumn colours had long gone from all the trees except the beeches to which still clung a few rags of brown leaf. It seemed impossible that these bare twigs and branches would, in a few months, be bursting into green and that even now the tight buds were moving imperceptibly to the swelling sap.

As I watched the river, I heard the quick whistle of a curlew and then a heron rose from one of the thin spits of golden sand that lay along its banks and with heavy wings flapped away upstream. I wondered how much damage the bird did to the fishing, for they are voracious feeders, and then I decided to follow its lead and go upstream.

The decision was a fortunate one. If anyone imagines that the English countryside is no more, and that there are now no places where it is possible to feel cut off entirely from the hum of cities and the ringing of telephone bells, let him follow the road which runs up the Wharfedale from Bolton Abbey, by Barden Bridge and Grassington and so to Kilnsey. I do not know the exact distance, perhaps eight miles, but there can be found no such eight miles anywhere else in England. The same might be said of many stretches of eight miles, that they are unique. How many such stretches would anyone want to travel again?

The road runs up and down the cliffs and scarps which overhang the river, and although at times dark woods hide the road and twisting hills seem to take you away from the river, it is never far distant. There is a variety of scenery, difficult to match. The broad valley pastures are cut by the winding river into curved jigsaw pieces, and the rising slopes of the fells that look down into the valleys are sometimes gentle and green, and sometimes steep and broken with the grey outcrops of limestone crag.

Now and then the road crosses the river by little bridges over which it is a crime to hurry, for such parapets were made to cushion stomachs as you look into the swift flow of brown water and watch for the glint of trout and grayling.

Anyone who can cross a Wharfedale bridge without wanting to stop and look over has little hope of discovering the real charm of this upland dale, where, as the innkeeper at Kilnsey told me, it is no uncommon thing for villages to be cut off from the world by snowdrifts for days at a time.

You should not miss that inn at Kilnsey. Its name, if I remember correctly, is the Kilnsey Arms, but it should be easy to find for it is the only one there. It faces the hurrying Wharfe, while behind it rises the sheer grey precipice of Kilnsey Crag, which reminded me for a moment of the cliffs at Cheddar. The building is unpretentious. Inside it is full of good things, and not the least is the conversation of the landlord and the men who sit in the chairs about the fire.

The room was empty, save for the landlord standing behind his curved bar, when I entered. I knew I had found a place of good cheer from the chairs. They were old, well-worn and had that comfortable look of belonging to a place, and I guessed that the men who had worn them to such a shine on the arms must be as interesting as the chairs looked. No one could sit in that bar and be out of temper for long. I sat there listening to the laughing landlord who, although he was not born a Yorkshire man, loves the county as much as the dalesmen who came into the bar, clapping their hands from the cold wind, and filling the room with gusts of talk and laughter and the fresh, bustling spirit of the dales.

I learned a great deal there about the ways of dalesmen and their love of their sheep and dogs before the landlord called me to my lunch which had been set in another room. At that time of year the hills were deserted of sheep for they had been taken down from the dales into the flat plain of eastern Yorkshire to feed on the richer pastures. There they stop until just before April, when they are brought back to the dales again for the lambing.

At the time of the annual exodus to the lowlands in September the roads are packed tightly with bleating flocks of sheep, barking dogs and sturdy drovers. If the ewes are kept on the fells the whole year round some deficiency in the feed causes their milk to dry up when the lambs come. To prevent this they are removed from the hills as soon as they have been served, or 'tupped' as the dales men call it. There is little rest for the dales men when the lambs come.

Shepherding is not the idyllic occupation suggested by some biblical illustrations. The shepherd has more to do than sit upon a hummock counting his sheep and occasionally going to search for straying lambs. Sheep have no great resistance to disease and a ewe may die suddenly behind some rock leaving two lambs to bleat for milk. Orphans have to be put to other ewes, and some ewes do not take kindly to orphans. When the lambs are old enough they have to be tailed, then there is the foot-rot and, with the warmer weather, the fly to watch, and then shearing... A summer's day for a shepherd is no lying in the grass watching the clouds and chewing a straw. He must for ever have his eyes on the flock, watching for that nervous movement which tells of a ewe with fly... and if you have ever seen a fleece working with fat white maggots, you will realise that it is no job for a squeamish man.

It was at this inn that I got, for a ridiculously small sum, a lunch which more than ever endeared me to Wharfedale, for after a man has had a morning full of beauty there is no better cap to it than a lunch which in itself is a thing of beauty. There was a rich, dark soup which was not only hot but full of the flavour of vegetables, then turkey with thyme and parsley stuffing, roast potatoes, Brussels sprouts, a fruit tart with a crust it was a shame to break and a joy to eat, a portion of Wensleydale cheese and a cup of as good a coffee as you could expect in England. I found it did not do to encourage the landlord's tabby with titbits. It misconstrued my lamentable kindness and leaped to the table to feed direct from the plate!

From Kilnsey I went on up the valley, branching right at Buckden, and climbed to the top of the Pennines through the tiny village of Cray, and it was here, on the saddle that leads down into Wensleydale, with the grim line of Buckden Pike overshadowing me, that I felt the true majesty of the hills.

Here was no attempt at prettiness; there was none of the fragility of the Cotswolds, or the purple distances of Dartmoor, only the barren sweeps of grass, the thick stone walls and the rough limestone crags. It was impossible to repress a feeling of awe and fear. I was standing alone on one of the great vertebrae of the backbone of England, above me the immensity of the sky and below, a complex, seething world, as frightening as the one above. I thought of Pascal and his imaginative conception of man standing between two immensities, above the universe, infinite and beyond the comprehension of human mind, and below that other universe in which the tiniest insect has all the complexity and activity of man himself. '*Le silence éternal de ces espaces infinis m'effraie.*' I wondered on what mountain-top he once stood between earth and sky and feared the immensities of loneliness and space. Perhaps on one of the crater-scarred tips of the mountains of his own Auvergne.

To my left and right might lie the turmoil of Lancashire and Yorkshire, but up here was a land which belonged to no county, was a region which owed allegiance only to the winds that ruled it and the cold, pale sky, all colour drawn from it by the bite of winter...

As I stood with the noise of the Gray Gill fall in my ears, whispering what might have been a protest at my intrusion, a bluster of wind swept down from the Pike and sprinkled me with snow. Here was a place, it seemed to howl at me, for grouse and sheep, for wheatear and hawk, but not for men.

I took the hint and hurried on my way down into Wensleydale, and now whenever I think of the Pennines I remember Wharfedale and the road that winds up and down by the river until it finally begins that steep climb to the head of the pass, where the most prosaic of men could not but feel that he has escaped 'from the contagion of the world's slow stain.'

CHAPTER 5

BETWEEN TWO RIVERS

It is not always wise to visit the places which one dreams about. I have never seen Mexico, though I have often longed to go there. Who would not want to go to a town with a name like Ciudad Las Casas?

But I am sure that the picture of Mexico which I have created in my mind (and my imagination has been aided by the films and the *National Geographic Magazine*) must be a gaudy exaggeration of the truth. And how many people on going to the towns which they have ringed with ink in a school atlas have wished they had never gone? This is an unfortunate human tendency. It is distressing to discover that the colourful image of the mind is so mundane and disappointing that it can never again be entitled to a place in the imagination.

These places of the mind exercise a queer fascination. Yet

it occasionally happens that the creation of your imagination is quite wrong and you are still delighted. Instead of finding a beautifully arranged garden you discover a luxuriant wilderness.

Until recently I had been to the Wirral peninsula only in imagination. There was something about that rectangular bluff of land lying between the rivers Dee and Mersey which always excited my interest when I looked at a map of England. I felt sure that it must be vastly different from anything else in England. I used to think about it at those times when I sat down with a map and planned journeys to places I had never seen. If you are very good at the game you even go so far as to look up train connections and enjoy yourself working out alternative routes in a Bradshaw, a book with more romance in it than many a modern novel, besides being cheaper. The Wirral... there was a medieval strain in the name, suggestive of long-bows and men in green. There it was on the map a stout, defiant barrier between the industrialism of Lancashire and the wild beauty of North Wales. I pictured the noble remains of the great oak forest which had once covered it, and all the shore that stretched beside the Dee gained a dim, eerie splendour in my fancies.

Now I have seen the Wirral and if I am offered a free trip to Mexico I am not sure whether I shall go. No! man is ever hopeful and I should go, but with some misgivings. My picture of the Wirral was wrong and I have not made up my mind whether the reality has disappointed or chastened me.

My own Wirral was too highly coloured and lacked any genuine shadows. The real Wirral is a substantial, material, illuminating place; a great natural, or unnatural, textbook on mankind, containing within a few square miles many types of human industry and desire.

When I got back from the Wirral I wrote an article on it which had been commissioned from me by the editor of a national daily newspaper. The article was never printed. The editor decided that it would be unwise to publish it. He was right. No paper can afford to offend a considerable section of its circulation. This may be a pitiable bar to truth, but nevertheless it exists. But what newspaper readers will not tolerate in newspapers they very often have to endure in books, for authors, from some unknown reason, have been given a greater measure of liberty than editors.

It may be that the man who has been annoyed by an author calling his town a stew reads on and gets a vicarious pleasure when the author throws other towns into the same pot. Again there is that sense of miraculous immunity which all readers enjoy. When George Bernard Shaw calls the English 'a race of constipated cow-eaters' you and I on reading this are quite sure that he does not mean specifically you and me, but the man next door and that awful Simpkins who bores us in the train and looks as though he never had any exercise in his life.

'Is the Wirral as gloomy as you make it?' asked the editor.

'It is,' I replied honestly.

'But there must be some beauty in it,' he insisted.

'I never said there wasn't. There is a great deal of beauty, of a kind. There is also much more ugliness.'

'Then write an article about the beauty alone.'

'And not mention anything about the ugliness?'

'Not if you can help it.'

I could not help it. It may be easy for those people who write town guides and advertisement pamphlets to omit the ugliness, after all that is part of their job and anyone with sense reads between the lines and knows that there is much omitted which could not have wisely been written. But I had been asked for my impressions. I went home and wrote another article, wrote two pages and then gave it up, for all the time the real Wirral was before my eyes, mocking the Wirral of my imagination on the paper. We decided that it might be better not to write about the Wirral. Some of the substance of that original article appears in the following pages and if you have any of the instinct of a great editor you will be able to identify it.

The sky was overcast with a grey pall of cloud while I was in the Wirral, but the greyness was nothing to the gloom which gradually swamped my soul. Never, I thought to myself, have I seen a district which exemplifies the prodigal and prodigious powers of man so shamefully. The whole district is one vast paradox, one gigantic contrast between man's powers for good and evil. At his best man is more industrious and efficient than any ant; at his worst there is no creature on this earth so stupid that it would be fair to compare it with man. The Wirral is a forcible example of man's two natures, the good and the bad, for the contrast between the Deeside and the Merseyside is not only remarkable, but saddening.

Here, on this peninsula, man has recognised in himself the twin desires to labour and to laugh, the need to work and the need to laze, and as such the Wirral is a sociological study no student of humanity should miss.

Before I saw them the sands of Dee had an appealing mystery which, I suspect, dates from the poetry readings of my schooldays. Mary calling the cattle home across the sands of Dee was a slightly pathetic and yet heroic figure, fit subject for one of those dark etchings you sometimes see in second-hand shops framed in a tawny wood; and I left Chester in a mood of expectation.

The country I travelled over was flat and cut into fields. All that remained of the great oak forest which I could see were the trees that lined the hedges, and their thick, tight-budded branches had a faintly mocking air in the winter light, as though they were deriding me for my imaginative simplicity. I was immune from derision before I had finished with the Wirral.

The oak forest has gone and its scattered survivors seem to have lost that essential Englishness of the oak and to have become no more than the accessories of a mocking, slightly macabre landscape. The peninsula coast on the Deeside is, in the south, fringed with long stretches of marsh, where flocks of sheep crop, as they do on the saltings of Norfolk, and seagulls float on the pools that litter the green of the marsh like scattered silver paper. Here and there a boat lies tilting high and dry, with its timbers rotting.

Far out beyond the rim of the marsh was the sea, hugged by a low blanket of mist and cloud that hid from me the distant Welsh mountains. There was a wildness and mystery in the long stretches of marsh which heightened my expectations of the rest of the coast.

I was disappointed. After the marshes come the famous sands, and in a few miles the loneliness of the first marshes and countryside gives way to a crowded colonisation. The Deeside has become a residential area, a succession of holiday resorts for the people of Birkenhead and its adjoining towns, and the whole stretch of coast has achieved a quite unique degree of ugliness. The country has disappeared under a litter of bungalows and shoddy houses in which even the few good buildings have their virtues obscured by the horror that crowds so closely around them. It is impossible to escape the awful houses and buildings.

Heswall, Thurstaston, West Kirby, Hoylake... they all have that same look and atmosphere. They are all places which should make a man stop and ponder upon the ugly effect of uncontrolled building. At one time there was beauty there. Indeed, there still is in fleeting patches. Then the great exodus from the cities on the other side of the peninsula began. People wanted to live in the country, by the seaside, and travel daily to their work in Liverpool and Wallasey, so they built themselves houses on the Dee. They built them hurriedly, a fault to be condoned sometimes, and they soon found themselves surrounded by other houses, built by other people who wanted to have fresh air and sea breezes, with the result that in no time the lovely views were obscured by brick walls and built over by other people seeking the freedom of the country. Nowadays I should prefer to live in the heart of Wallasey rather than anywhere on that coast of Dee.

There is one place on the Dee which has escaped some of man's awful eagerness, and that is Parkgate. Here, for a moment, it was almost possible to imagine that I was in some Cornish fishing village. Rows of small boats and yachts swung at anchor, gulls screamed in wild clouds over my head, and at the end of the promenade stood a group of fishermen in yellow oilskins and sea-boots. The buildings along the front were pleasantly white in contrast to the grey-green sea. I was tempted to speak to the fishermen, but I resolved not to do so. I was still suffering from my disappointment with the coast and did not wish to risk another.

The Deeside has become a playground for hundreds after the toil and strain of a Birkenhead week, and a haven for those workers who are able to afford to live away from the towns where they work. I could not help feeling what a terrible pity it was that this admirable resolution to get away into the country and to the seaside should have been pursued with such enthusiasm that very soon the conditions from which the families were removing were being recreated around them. We cannot all live in the country, although most of us would like to, and the people who do live in places which enjoy a lovely isolation and freedom from the presence of cities may wonder at our joy when we are able to get away from the welter of buildings and tramways into the peace of a suburb. Many of the places in the peninsula are suburbs of the large industrial areas, and to hundreds they represent the country and freedom from smoke and grime. That these places are now losing the charm and peace they once held out to tired business men and wives anxious for the green of fields is a tragedy, and the blame belongs to no one in particular and yet it belongs to every person living in the peninsula. If the dwellers by the Dee want to preserve the rural beauties which drew them from Birkenhead and Liscard they must do it themselves – and do it soon. If they do not the time is not far distant when they will begin to long for the peaceful industrialism of Birkenhead, twenty minutes away.

The appeal of the peninsula lies more in its human interest than any natural or historical features. On the Deeside are the famous sands, littered with cigarette cartons and fronted by an almost continuous growth of houses which I shall not be sorry if I do not see again. And then there is the Merseyside, a vital, dominating place where it is never impossible to find something interesting and stimulating.

There is no pretension on the Merseyside. It is frankly industrial and commercial, and the sprawling masses of houses, factories and docks which are Wallasey, Liscard and Birkenhead offer no excuses for their ugliness. There is no doubt about the feeling of these towns. It is here that work is done, and everywhere is a frankness of purpose that mitigates the ugliness, and even achieves beauty in the gaunt jibs of cranes and about the busy traffic of ships lying in dock. There is always the continuous flow of sea – traffic up and down the river and at Eastham Ferry is the beginning of that great engineering masterpiece, the Manchester Ship Canal. It is surprising that the same people who have produced the dignity of the Merseyside should also have perpetrated the urban monotony of the rest of the district, for it is literally true that the whole of the peninsula has become a suburb of Liverpool and Birkenhead.

In Birkenhead it was slightly disconcerting to discover in the middle of the town, after wandering around acres of dingy streets, the entrance to the Mersey tunnel, an omnivorous mouth guarded by coloured pay-boxes and sentinelled by a tall black column, decorated in an Egyptian fashion that struck a bizarre note amongst the dirty buildings of the rest of the town.

As I stood by the tunnel a couple of Lascars from some ship walked by me and stood staring a while at the gilded column and the dark tunnel mouth. They were undersized, thin men, dressed in crumpled reach-me-downs and wearing caps too large for them. They had that timid, chastened air which characterises poorer orientals in a foreign city. They stood for a moment eyeing the tunnel and I wondered if each time they came off ship at Birkenhead they walked solemnly to this place to pay silent homage to the one touch of the Orient in the town.

I lost myself several times in the maze of Birkenhead's streets. One thing I could not lose and that was the docks; Birkenhead has been a shipbuilding town since the beginning of the nineteenth century and the feeling of ships and the sea is everywhere.

It was from the great Laird yard here that the ill-fated *Alabama* sailed in 1862, during the American Civil War. The *Alabama*, a disguised privateer, was allowed to sail from Birkenhead, despite the fact that the United States consul at Liverpool had acquainted the authorities with her real character. For two years she harried the shipping of the Northern States until she was sunk off Cherbourg. That she had ever been allowed to sail was a direct breach of England's neutrality. It also showed how ignorant of American feeling were the statesmen of that time. 'If Lord John (Russell) had known Boston society as well as he knew the Italian exiles,' says G. M. Trevelyan, 'he would have taken a little more trouble than he did to prevent the sailing of the *Alabama*.' And he would have saved England, and future tax-payers, the enormous claim of over three million pounds which was awarded against her ten years later by an international court of arbitration.

From the Laird yard, in 1829, came the first iron ship ever launched in England, to mark the beginning of the mythical Mother Shipton's prophecy that 'iron should float and carriages without horses run.'

I wanted lunch while I was in Birkenhead, and I asked a policeman to direct me to a good cafe.

'You won't do better than that,' he said, nodding across the roadway to where a notice was fixed to the railings of a tall house.

I thanked him, and crossing the road, went down the area steps which led to the cafe. I found myself in a large room, lit by two windows that looked out into the well of the area and brightened by the polish on the brass utensils which hung upon the walls. At the far end of the room a huge kitchen range smiled the blackest and shiniest smile I have ever seen. I knew that I was in a place where I should be well satisfied for a few people, obviously regular patrons, looked at me with the scarce-hidden annoyance which comes over one's face at the intrusion of a stranger into one's favourite cafe. In Birkenhead, the city of the tunnel, perhaps all good things are found underground.

At the next table were two young men and it was obvious from their talk, which I could not help but hear, that they were actors met for a while in Birkenhead before passing on with their respective companies. Their talk was mostly of common acquaintances, and went like this:

'What's happened to Charlie these days?

'Never hear anything about him.'

'Him? Oh – is that French mustard? Pass it would you? Him, he's left the stage now. Keeps a fish and chip shop in Plymouth – married the daughter, I think. Bit of funny business about that if you ask me. I shall get the inside story when we play Exeter. Remember Johnny Crew and his craze for playing Shakespeare with Benson?'

'You bet. He was in rep. with me for a while at Blackpool. What's he doing?'

'Chorus in an Edinburgh panto. He's a card.'

'I'll say he is. I shall never forget the night when he and...'

What they were doing, whether they were both playing that night in the same or separate theatres at Birkenhead, or Liverpool, I never found out. There was something pathetic in the eagerness with which they exchanged news. It might be months, years before they met, or perhaps they never would meet again. The stage, especially for those conscientious, aspiring, but never-to-be-famous men and women who serve the provinces, is a hard master.

When I left they were still talking hard, but they had exhausted their news and were swapping jokes...

From Birkenhead I went on to Port Sunlight. Port Sunlight, not far from Birkenhead, must be seen to be believed. An oasis in a morass of industry, it is a classical example of benevolent capitalism, and a demonstration of the power of soap. The hundreds of houses, quartered by fresh greens and walks, represent all styles of English cottage architecture. Its abiding merit is that the architects have not attempted to reproduce all the styles in one house as is done in some suburban estates.

I saw happier, healthier-looking people in Port Sunlight than anywhere else in the Wirral, and now every time I wash my hands I feel that the act is one of blessing, for it perpetuates in the Wirral a beauty which deserves a more appreciative audience.

When you go to the Wirral you may not be as disappointed as I was. If you have read these words you will not be expecting so much as I was. Maybe you will find there much that I missed, or see in places which appalled me an interest which holds you. I hope so, for I would like to think that my view was jaundiced and that the district deserves better than I have given it.

If your faith in the sanity of mankind is shaken; if you cannot reconcile the stupidity of the Dee with the dirty dignity of the Mersey then wander along the Mersey shore, passing the explosive and margarine factories, tripping over railway lines and trespassing upon factory roads until you come to Eastham Ferry where the canal begins, and in the public house there you will find good beer and conversation with men who love the dirty Mersey in a way which is past explanation, and if you are in no mood for talk, you can lean upon the fence overlooking the entrance to the canal and watch the great ships come out of the mist to pass inland, a dim, silent procession.

CHAPTER 6

THE POTTERIES

Dr Johnson, in an idle moment, during his tour of the Hebrides with Boswell, once composed a meditation upon a pudding. The meditation, while it makes good reading, is a bad recipe. I fancy Dr Johnson's pudding would be as ponderous as he was and would weigh heavier upon one than his devastating retorts. The meditation is enough to show that a pudding has in it those elements which must excite all men's wonder and is such a compound of creative mysteries that it almost becomes a sacrilege to eat it.

It is a pity that Dr Johnson, although he was born at Lichfield, so close to the Potteries, did not visit them with his Boswell and give us a meditation upon a basin, for there is in the making of a basin enough speculative material to satisfy anyone, and perhaps the basin deserves a more noble meditation than the pudding, for without the basin where would the pudding be?

If without the basin the pudding is lost, or at the best wrapt in the sorry folds of a cloth to lose its flavour, then without the Potteries they are both lost. That so much which is essential to mankind's happiness should depend upon so curious a district is a fit subject for reflection.

Judged from any standard the Potteries district is ugly. Yet it is not an ugliness which repels. It challenges deliberate attention with its frankness and seems to cry aloud from every pot-bank and street: 'We may be ugly and dirty, but that is because we work, because we have a task that makes us what we are.'

The honesty of this cry may be judged from the fact that the Potteries does not, as so many other industrial areas do, overrun into the surrounding countryside in sprawling, shapeless islands and peninsulas of ugliness, but gathers itself into one compact district. It restrains its red-bricked horror within rigid bounds, as though it sensed the contamination which it bears and were reluctant to touch more than it need. There is no intermediate sordidness of patchy settlements, half residential and half industrial, between the Potteries and the countryside. Where the Potteries cease the real country begins.

On a day when most farmers were thinking of the lambing that was to come, I stood upon a hillside, surrounded by sheep and shivering in a wind that swept across from the barren Peak district. In a few months, I thought, there would be thyme and bugle in the bare grass, and stonecrop and toadflax rioting over the stone walls. Now there was only the yellow grass and the dark stems of dead nettles. High above me a hawk hovered and across a neighbouring field a horse and cart moved slowly as a farm-hand pitched out swedes for cattle fodder. I might have been on some moorland farm, miles from the nearest town. I was not. When I turned round, across the valley behind me, I could see the Potteries.

Instead of sheep, long rows of houses covered the hillside and mixed with them were the lines of kilns, chimneys and the occasional spire of a church. No hawk moved in the wind; there were instead the plumes of smoke from the chimneys and the slow journey of a conveyor carrying refuse to a mountainous slag heap along an overhead wire.

No matter where you go in the County Borough of Stoke-on-Trent, which embraces all the Potteries and includes more than just the five towns of Arnold Bennett, this is the typical outlook. It is a landscape, painted in red and grey, of 'pot-banks,' as the potteries are called, coal pit and steelwork. Everywhere are chimneys and the narrow-necked kilns, like huge, dirty milk jars, and thrusting up here and there are heaps of slag and refuse.

The streets are not narrow. They are dismal and uninspired, and their lighting, to anyone accustomed to the glare of London, seems worse than niggardly. In Hanley and Burslem there are fine modern shops, filled with a wealth of bright clothes and polished furniture. The red brick admits no rival, and the concrete purity of the modern shops and buildings is quickly discounted by the weight of red-bricked houses and the steep roads paved with dingy brown sets. It was with surprise that I noticed the modern buildings after I had been in the district for some time, for my eyes were occupied with the kilns, those emblems of the Potteries' real life, where earthenware is glossed and baked, and the flints which are used in the manufacture of pottery are calcined.

The district is hilly and no space is left uncovered. Coalmine, steel-work, pot-bank and tile factory crouch in the valleys and along the hillsides, streets and shops take what they can.

Nowhere did I see a children's playground and, even if there are any, as I have no doubt there must be, the children seem to prefer playing at street corners under the light of the lamps, but that is a perversity of child nature which is found even in the greenest towns.

I was shown over one of the pot-banks. I stood for a while in the porter's room at the main entrance, talking with the porter and warming myself at his fire. As we stood there a policeman came in, nodded to the porter and said:

'May I use the telephone?'

'Ay, you may,' answered the porter. The policeman picked up the instrument and called his superintendent at the police station.

'Sergeant — speaking. There's a swan up here on the canal,' he said, 'with a broken wing and it looks as though it's dying. Been like it for a couple of days. What shall I do?'

He was silent listening to his superior's instructions about the dying swan and while he stood there, his head cocked to the earpiece, I was called away to begin my tour of the pottery. I asked the porter as I left if he knew what the policeman had decided to do, but he shook his head. No one admires the police more than I do for their efficiency and I should like to have known exactly what their procedure would be with a dying swan with a broken wing. Here was a missed opportunity, too, for me to put to the test the fable of the death song of the dying swan...

The foreman who showed me over the works left no doubt in my mind of the pride which these people take in their industry. It is not just their bread and butter, a job which they do for so many hours a day and then forget when they reach home. It is their life, and they are not ashamed to admit it.

He showed me the whole process from beginning to end, and his manner reminded me of my schooldays.

'This is the canal wharf where the boats come from the Mersey bringing clay from Dorset and Devon. It is put into trucks and runs along that overhead rail and is then shot into these different stalls, according to the type of clay. Mind your head as you go down here. See, the brown clay in that stall comes from Dorset – we use that for one kind of crockery. The white clay, or kaolin in the other stall comes from Dartmoor and is used for other work...'

There was no need for him to tell me that the white china clay came from Dartmoor. As a boy I had lived in Plymouth and if any boy who lives in Plymouth has walked out to Plym Bridge, blackberrying, or to fish for tadpoles, and not stolen a ride home on the top of a china clay wagon coming down from the moor – then he is no boy at all. The ride back behind a horse patiently pulling a string of wagons filled with white clay was always an adventure, for the carters were not over-fond of small boys... His voice woke me from my reverie.

'This series of magnets set across the running sludge removes all the particles of steel which come into it during the various processes. It is essential to get this out, otherwise in the baking the steel would discolour the crockery and probably crack it.'

With the care – and patience – of a mother explaining a moral lesson to a child, he took me through the works; from the canal where the clay came in, to the kilns where the calcined flints lay in whitey-grey heaps, and where, in earthenware tubs, the clay cups and plates were packed to be glossed by the action of the heat on the minerals sprinkled over them.

I do not think he would have minded had I not been listening as he explained the various processes. It was when we came to the 'slip' that I realised that I was in the presence of a master. The 'slip' is the prepared clay, ready for shaping into cup, plate, or any other china object. All the excess water squeezed from it by gigantic presses, it travels from the final mixing machine in a long strip, like paste being forced from an enormous tube.

'Look at that,' he said, his voice rising and his face suddenly bright with a new expression. He leaned over and sliced a piece of slip from the length with a wire, much as a grocer cuts cheese. 'Isn't that grand stuff?' he asked, and shook his head as his fingers played and dug into the soft clay. 'It's good enough to eat.' And all the while he spoke his fingers were playing with the clay, fingering, caressing and shaping it. He was a mild-mannered, undistinguished man, but in that moment I realised that it was not just clay he was handling, but vivid, living stuff without which his life would be nothing, and as he fingered it there was a light in his eyes which probably few other things in this world could evoke. I was suddenly awed before him, as we must all be awed before a craftsman. In that moment, as I stood there watching the long line of clay ooze from the mixing machine, I regretted that I had not been born in the Potteries and become a potter. Here was a man who worked with his hands, knew a craft shared by a comparative few and one that was as old as mankind. He had every right to be arrogant, to scorn me and the rest of the world, I felt. As he stood there he represented, as faithfully as anyone I have ever met and with a beauty that was impossible to forget, the dignity of labour and the pride which comes from having a craft.

And all around there were others who felt the same, who shared a like spirit. To the people of the Potteries clay is not something from which they make a living, it is their life. The girls working in the pot-banks, whether they do no more than carry long tray-fulls of cups from the drying-rooms to the kilns, or paint those coloured bands round the plates, or stick transfers on the cheaper china, all seem to have this feeling for the trade they own, a trade as old as any in the world; and the men and boys all have a joy in their work which comes from a heritage of craftsmanship. When I had first seen them at night, dressed-up, laughing and jostling in picture queues, out to enjoy themselves, I had not guessed at their pride, but when I saw them in that pot-bank I should have had to have been imperceptive to have missed it.

The history of the Potteries is a history of individuals. The Dutch brothers, Elers, are the first in the line of individuals who raised the craft from an unimportant occupation of a few at Burslem, the mother of the Potteries, to the position of a major industry. About 1690 these brothers discovered a vein of clay near Bradwell Wood from which they produced a fine red stoneware and, most important, they introduced into the industry the secret of making the famous salt-glazed stoneware. So jealous were they of this secret that it is said, with what truth you must judge for yourself, that the two brothers employed none but half-wits in their pot-banks so that they might not discover the secret or communicate it to other people, and every day – as though they were not sure even of their half wits – all the workmen were searched before they left the factory.

And after the Elers brothers came Josiah Wedgwood who, as the inscription on his monument reads: '...converted a rude and inconsiderable manufactory into an elegant art and an important part of national commerce.'

Josiah Wedgwood's chief genius lay in his love of experiments. Born in the Potteries of a family which had for years been engaged in the trade, after he had served his apprenticeship with his brother, Thomas, he was refused a partnership because of his unorthodox experiments. Josiah, like so many other famous inventors, was too progressive for the men of his own age. Yet it is of him that most people think when pottery is mentioned, and when you are in the Potteries you will hardly fail to miss Etruria, the village and factory which he founded for the manufacture of cream-coloured earthenwares, black basaltes and jasper ware, all of which he introduced or improved by his experiments. He had that high courage which comes from faith, and from his faith he helped to build one of the greatest and most interesting industries in the world.

Anyone in the Potteries, I found, can tell you about the Wedgwood family and the two Ralph Woods, who made the sometimes crude, but always humorous, Staffordshire figures. Yet there was one name which produced no response from quite a lot of people. Ask a Potteries man or woman anything you like about their jobs and you will have a ready answer. Ask them if they have ever heard of Arnold Bennett, and do not be surprised if they look at you with polite blankness.

CHAPTER 7

THE SMALLEST OF THE FAMILY

What is there about small things which excites our interest and our sympathy, and evokes an excess of kindness which takes control of us before we have time to be ashamed of it?

Sheep are dull, stupid creatures, which in flocks achieve a certain picturesqueness, but individually have little interest save for their shepherd. Is there any man or woman, however, who has not felt something stir within at the sight of a young spring lamb, butting at its fellows and arching its back in tiny leaps? Grace, beauty and overflowing life; it has them all to make us feel happier at the sight of it. Kittens; fluffed-up young thrushes, trying their wings for the first time; a puppy working itself into a frenzy as it chases its own tail… is there anyone so occupied with his own cares that he cannot stop to smile at these small creatures?

We can always find a place in our heart for the smallest of things, and if I love Rutland it is perhaps because it is our smallest county, and not so large that a man cannot come to know it without years of exploration. Yorkshire we must love in parts. It is too vast to claim an entire affection. England is so small that to love part of it is to love all of it.

If anyone asked me which county in England is least spoiled, I should answer without hesitation – Rutland. In some miraculous way it has escaped the horrors which have attacked other counties. Its greatest quality is its unobtrusiveness. There is nothing to excite or alarm you in Rutland. It still retains that quiet leisurely English atmosphere which was typical of the eighteenth century. It would not have surprised me to have discovered a Rutland Sir Roger de Coverley leading his grumbling parishioners to church and daring any to sleep through the sermon but himself, or that the cottage wives flout the aid of modern therapeutics and give the juice of crushed snails to their children to cure them of whooping cough, or prescribe a dish of minced mice to ward off the Evil One.

I cannot tell you where to go and what to see in Rutland, for there is nowhere to go and nothing to see. If you want to understand Rutland you must just go to any village, picked out at random, and there leave your bicycle, bus or motor car and without consulting a map strike away in the direction which appeals most to you. You will never be disappointed. Within a mile you will be lost in old England, an England where the news of the battle at Bunker's Hill in faraway America might still be being told from cottage to cottage, where the only sounds to disturb the peace of the morning were the sudden winding of a hunting horn from a copse and the crisp beat of hooves across dead grass...

Somewhere in the county there is a little, grey-stoned cottage, not unlike the cottages of the Cotswolds, with sprays of yellow jasmine guarding the doorway, and friendly hens pecking between the unfolding daffodils of the flower-beds, while from the roof pent white fantails pursue their courtships with more noise than nicety.

I cannot tell you where the cottage is – for I do not know. I only know that it is somewhere in Rutland, and that when I first saw it I welcomed it with all the joy of a wanderer. I was lost. This may appear impossible, but in Rutland it very easily happens. For what seemed like hours I went along narrow roadways and lanes, twisting up wooded heights and dipping down into wide river-paved valleys. Once I came to a small village that straggled along the roadway, graced by a tiny, untidy green where a donkey was grazing half-heartedly, ignoring the persistent attentions of two small boys.

I went into the post office to enquire my way to Oakham and found that I had wandered right out of Rutland and was in Northamptonshire. Rutland is an elusive county. One minute you are in it and the next – you are away in Leicestershire or Lincolnshire.

I was soon lost again for I tried to take a short cut on the advice of the postmistress...

When I found the cottage I was despairing of ever reaching Oakham at all. I wish all lost travellers such a happy ending to their wanderings as I found in that cottage.

At my knock on the door it was opened by a large genial woman. She wore a blue-and-white print overall, and her hair was piled on her head in an old-fashioned bun and her face was obviously the face of a woman who loved children, animals and anything which had strayed. I came into the last category and, almost before I had finished explaining that I was lost, that I was thirsty, and that I wanted to get to Oakham, she had taken me in hand.

I was conducted through a low room, full of plush-framed pictures and photographs, with a mantelshelf burdened by a vase of imitation chenille flowers, to a kitchen that smelt of cleanliness, and soon I was washing myself under a tap.

'Freshen yourself up there, my dear,' she said and disappeared. It was a hot spring day and I needed that wash. And afterwards I sat in the wooden porch-way, with the sun cutting slants of golden-moted light across the shadows and slaked my thirst; but not with draughts of well-water, or the proverbial glass of milk fresh from the cow, or even the herby homemade beer which the cottagers of the Peak district love to force upon one. No, Rutland is a homely English county and I was given tea, and I wanted nothing else. Whilst I drank and smoked my pipe and tried to stop one of a horde of black kittens from drowning itself in my cup, the good lady told me about her life and her garden.

'It's lonely here at times,' she said, 'for the master's away most of the day. I find me company in the animals and the garden, though.' As she spoke she relieved me of the kitten which was about to make another attempt in my cup. The 'master' was her husband, who was a hedger and ditcher.

'You like animals?' I asked.

She nodded. 'They take the place of children with me. There's the pigeons, the kittens – I don't know where the old lady is. She's away mousing in the barns very likely. And Sarah, our bitch that is, she's away today with the master. She's due for her pups soon. It keeps a house lively to have young things around –'

To have young things around – I wondered what sorrow lay behind her words.

'Then there's always the garden,' she went on. 'Master does the kitchen garden at the back when he comes home and I look after the flowers. You should come and see the garden in the summer. It's a real picture. That's the one thing I want to go to London for. I suppose you've been to Kew Gardens many a time?'

I nodded.

'They say it's a rare sight. Maybe if I went and saw it I should feel dissatisfied with our little plot here.'

I thought of Kew and wondered if she would feel dissatisfied, and I was afraid she might for a while, though I doubt whether Kew could ever mean as much to anyone as her garden meant to her.

It was while I sat there, resting and enjoying the sunshine, that I realised for the first time that spring had really come. She always comes with a burst, and there is a moment when we open our eyes and acknowledge her presence with a cry of surprise. And at that moment in the porch-way spring came to Rutland.

Not far away a dark-coloured stream rushed by in spate, the green flags dipping and bowing in the current. Over the water hung a tall willow, the light through its young leaves turning it into a waving wonder. Everywhere the leaves were bursting their bud cases; blackthorn, sycamore and hazel were all alive again and hiding the dark tracery of their boughs with the brightness of their foliage. Only the beech and ash still lay wrapped tightly in their close buds. In the hedge at the bottom of the garden were stippled the tiny white faces of whitlow grass and faintly on the breeze came the scent of violets, which I knew were hiding under their dark leaves in the ditch by the roadside... spring had come.

The chestnuts flaunted a thousand tiny green cloaks, the arum pushed its fleshy finger towards the light, and in the straw and fur-lined burrows young rabbits were moving in sightless struggles. The chaffinches sang while the busier hedge-sparrow already had found its nesting site and was building. The moorhens by the river clucked about the reeds on the same errand, the fantails on the roof rumbled in their crops about the spring and the good lady by my side sat eyeing her garden, looking at the purple glory of her violas, and in her eyes was a light which seemed not to have been there a moment before...

I shall always remember Rutland for that moment. It is a county of hidden villages and cottages, full of drowsiness and peace, of fields so vast that it has been said that the smallest county has the largest fields, and everywhere there is an atmosphere that is English, solid and sincere. Nowhere was there any bustle or hurry. I saw no theatres, no cinemas, and only one train puffing quietly up an incline. Even the Great North Road, which cuts across a corner of the county, alters its character for a while and plays at being a country road, and the cars which whizz up and down it slacken speed as though the drivers sensed the peace and were anxious not to disturb it with their haste.

The most noise I heard in Rutland came from a group of schoolchildren outside a hall in Oakham, the capital of the county. They were excited and dancing with impatience, and I learnt that they had come in from the surrounding villages for a musical festival.

At the inn, where I lunched in Oakham, the talk in the bar was not of government and politics, but of racecourses, of crops and the ways of hounds and horses. It was the day of the Grand National, and there were few people in the bar.

'This is always a quiet day for us,' said the landlord. 'I wish I could have gone, but a man must look after his business these days.'

'You mean you would have gone if you could have left your wife at home,' said a horsey-looking man who was drinking his beer by the window. 'She wouldn't trust you alone on a racecourse.'

The landlord laughed good-humouredly. 'It's the train fare – not the wife.'

'You should do the same as Billy, then,' came the reply.

'Who is Billy?' I asked and was told.

Billy is a groom and for years he has never missed a Grand National. Never having enough money to pay for his railway fare, or perhaps not wishing to waste on railway fare what he can put on a horse, Billy leaves Rutland on his bicycle every year on the day before the Grand National and cycles towards Liverpool. Whether he spends his night under a hedge or in a cheap lodging depends upon his finances. He leaves his bicycle at a cottage a few miles from the course, and then finishes his journey on foot. He sees the races, loses or wins money, and cycles back home. His homeward journey is cheerfully erratic, or monotonously virtuous according to his luck at the races. Yet, no matter what his fortune, he always arrives back at Oakham with empty pockets. I should like to have met Billy – he seems to have a philosophy which is not too common these days.

Yes, the modern world has passed Rutland by. At any moment packs of tail-waving hounds crowd the roadway and the thud of hunters is heard across the pastures, while along the crests of the fields there is always the eternal silhouette of men behind ploughs. The quality, which Rutland possesses more than any other county, of peace and contentment is enduring and unassailable. Rutland will be Rutland whatever happens, and there will always be somewhere a cottage like mine where hospitality is not a forgotten word, but a real, vital thing which breaks down all barriers and keeps alive a spirit which is all kindness and humanity.

Someday I am going back to that cottage to drink tea again – if I can find it in the maze of grey villages with their short-spired churches and the spread of fields and valleys.

CHAPTER 8

FENLAND TOWN

From Charles Kingsley I know all about Hereward the Wake and the Fens. Is there anyone who does not? Is there anybody who has read that saga of the last stand of the Saxons against the invading Normans, who has not felt in his heart a thrill of pride and a feeling of gratitude towards that corner of the land where dauntless men and women resisted the invaders, resisted and finally triumphed?

William the Conqueror made an honourable peace with the last Saxons; but it was not the Saxons who had worn down his sallies and disheartened his armies – it was the fens, those grim, treacherous, sedgy wastes, which had conquered.

And today the fens themselves have been conquered and enslaved. If you go to the district expecting to see acres of marshes tufted with spikes of reed, cut into deep waterways where monstrous pike lie in the shadows and squadrons of wildfowl nest – you will be disappointed.

Except for a few patches the real fens have disappeared. Beet, corn, potatoes and peas have ousted the reeds and water-flowers, and the meres and swamps have been schooled into drains and dykes where the fish and wildfowl, their numbers diminished by time, still linger.

The lonely figure that bends to the dark earth, taking his living from the fields, had ancestors who moved about the wild fens with their long jumping poles, living on the duck and fish; and the fat-bellied monk who stood beside the Ouse at Ely watching the grain-boats being poled towards the landing stages, has given way to an aesthetic-looking cleric who steps from his train on to the railway platform at Ely, holding a heavy, illustrated edition of *Ecclesiastes* under his arm.

March means to you a month which comes in like a lion and generally does its best to go out like one, despite the old adage. March used to mean that to me until I went to the fens and discovered another; the town of March.

It lies in the heart of the fen country, not far from the tip of the Wash, and it was to March that I went on a day in early spring, when that season was trying to emulate the royal colours of summer, handicapped by a less plentiful palette and an unaccustomed hand. The sky was a pale, washed blue, with a fluffy fringe of clouds circling the horizon in a faint, untidy halo.

I walked along a road bordered by a deep drain, as the fen people prosaically name the rivers and dykes that cut the country into angular islands. Why a waterway, which is as good as a river in this district, should be called 'Sixteen Foot Drain' or 'Twenty

Foot Drain' instead of having a name which is no more than a mathematical index to its size, is a mystery which has a solution in the minds of those able, but obviously unromantic persons who first reclaimed the fen country into arable land. To see the words 'Main Drain' running alongside a tempting stream of blue on a map is enough to make any walker unused to the names of the district, draw quite wrong conclusions and give it a miss.

The drain that ran by the road was confined within banks as steep as a railway cutting, and brown with the dead litter of hogweeds. It flowed with a steady, purposeful motion towards the far meeting of sky and fields. The countryside might have been formed by some geometric titan. All straightness and sharp angles, an endless vista of flatness, broken now and again by a few elms or poplars, it is an area which forces you into an awareness of the sky, for there is little to hold the eye to the earth.

To walk along the flat fen roads is agony, since you can see your destination an hour before you come to it. I could see the tower of March's town hall long before I reached the town. To cycle along the roads in a head wind is a heart-breaking task, and to drive is to invite an insidious monotony which, if unrepulsed, will have you in a ditch before you know where you are. Even the men who made the roads and drains must have tired of the eternal straightness. There are at times unaccountable twists and curves that merely emphasise the monotony.

A plough moved across the hedgeless field at my side and a cloud of gulls hung behind it in a noisy worrying wake, fighting over the leather jackets and grubs turned up in the tilth. The gulls come inland from the Norfolk coast and the Wash, following the ploughs and searching the furrows by day, and quartering in restless squadrons on the dykes and open meres by night.

As far as I could see there was chocolate-coloured earth lying ready for the seed or already showing faint lines of young green. Only the occasional belts of trees, black filigrees against the sky, broke the flatness, and on a tiny mound in the middle distance stood a disused windmill, like a fantastic pepper-pot.

And so I came to March, an oasis in the flatness. March has grown since those early days when the fen-men settled, for safety from the floods and for companionship, on the slight rise by the muddy shores of the River Nene. Some people have said that it is more a museum piece than a town, but they were modernists, who are never happy unless a town has a traffic problem and enough cinemas to provide a different bill for each of the seven nights of the week. March is modern enough; it has its chain stores, its cinemas and banks, but over all there is the still, deep spirit of the fens. The town offers security from the lonely vistas and dark monotony of the huge fields. The houses, inns and churches cluster about the long main street as though the men who built them were moved by the thought that to be denied companionship in this flat, bleak country was almost to be denied life.

A middle-aged man whom I talked to on the town bridge explained his feeling to me.

'Maybe it's not a beautiful town,' he admitted, 'but it's clean and friendly. That's more than you could say for a lot of other bigger places. And you'll find no slums here.' He shook his head sagely and looked over into the green river.

The river at March is an outcast. In most towns which are fortunate enough to be placed on a river, the position is used to advantage and the river performs a score of useful functions. In March there is no good word to be said for the river. There is no boating on it, little fishing and less bathing, it drives no mill, and helps no laundry. In the wintertime it is a dark brown, turgid stream, overhung by the wan skeletons of a few willows, while in the summer it loses what little current it possesses and although the willows drop cascades of feathery branches towards the water, they find there no answering loveliness, for the lack of current lets a green scum coat the top of the stream, and in midsummer an unpleasant odour arises from this stagnation which affronts a stranger crossing the bridge and disgusts the inhabitants.

With a little effort on the part of the town council, or the river authorities, March could be graced by a stream which might be her greatest beauty. As it is, she is not only disgraced by it, but often literally put out of countenance.

Architecturally the main buildings are not distinguished. The town hall is a sorry red-brick creation from which the bronze Britannia, who surmounts its tower, averts her eyes with certain justice. Opposite the town hall is the creeper-clad length of the Griffin Inn, one of the most comfortable and pleasant inns in England. Elsewhere, as I passed about the town, I came across glimpses of pleasant Queen Anne and Georgian houses, though March cannot rival its near neighbour Wisbech for eighteenth-century houses. March is growing and has its sporadic outbursts of new houses, but the real March clusters about the river where are the thatched roofs of the old cottages, and the blackened timbers of the Ship Inn, one of the oldest inns in Cambridgeshire.

At first I did not imagine that March had little to distinguish it from a hundred other small country towns. I was wrong. I had not been there long before I became aware that mixed among the ordinary people in the street was a surprising number of men in blue overalls, wearing black peaked caps and carrying dinner-pails. They were, I discovered, railwaymen.

March was, I was told with a great deal of pride, an important railway junction, and possessed the largest marshalling yard in Europe.

'What,' I asked, 'is a marshalling yard?'

The railway official I was speaking to winced and then said quietly: 'Perhaps you had better come and see for yourself. It is rather difficult to explain in words to anyone who doesn't know much about railways.'

I rather resented the imputation that I knew nothing about railways. I covered my feelings and followed him. It was growing dusk when we came to the yards. Before me were what seemed to be miles and miles of railway lines, as though all the sidings in the country had gathered together for a conference. Here and there were strings of trucks, clanging behind panting engines; a searchlight poked its long finger through the dusk at us, and inside a square tower in the centre of the yards lights suddenly sprang into being.

'Come with me,' I was told, and I followed, stumbling across the dim lines and climbed into the tower. The room at the top was walled with glass so that a view of the whole yards swept before me as I turned round. It reminded me of a ship's bridge and the inside of a signal box. There were shining levers, wheels, a loudspeaker that bellowed orders, and winking red and green lights. I listened while the mechanism was explained to me. I have not a mechanical mind. When my car goes wrong, if cleaning the plugs and tickling the carburettor does not remedy the trouble, I call in the garage man. The technical account which was given to me of the mechanism of the marshalling yard was remarkable for the recurrence of the words 'automatic' and 'Westinghouse brakes.'

You are still probably wondering what a marshalling yard is; or wondering why I am taking so much time to describe something which is common knowledge to everyone of intelligence. For the sake of the few who do not know, and in order to clarify my own information I will try to explain – but not in technical language.

Have you ever wondered how a truck of coal from Durham finally reaches a coal merchant's siding in Dorchester? I never had until I went to March. And it is March which is mainly responsible for the truck getting to Dorchester and not Doncaster. A goods train comes puffing down from Durham with trucks consigned to various towns. It reaches March and there the trucks, with hundreds of others, are shunted up on to a high embankment in 'runs' of about fifty trucks. The end of the embankment slopes towards the yards and splits into a number of separate lines. Imagine your arm to be the high embankment with a railway line running along it towards your wrist and then imagine your fingers to be the duplication of that one line into many others. The truck from Durham for Dorchester runs down the arm, bumps across the points at the wrist, which are controlled by the men in the tower, and glides away down your little finger into the bay for all Dorchester trucks. Behind it is a truck for Bath which shoots down into your thumb, which is the bay for Bath traffic. And so the shunting goes on all day and all night at March, hundreds of trucks passing down the incline and into their respective bays. The bays are not always for separate towns. Sometimes they are for districts, like the West of England, or London; but all goods traffic coming from the North for the South passes through a sifting process at March. It is a keen railway brain that controls goods traffic. Loudspeakers boom instructions over the yards to the brake men (and sometimes send out unofficial information about the winner of the four-thirty), arc-lights pick out the thin weft of steel lines, signals clank up and down, and the passing furnace of an engine shows driver and stoker like a couple of unfortunates in a tiny hell of their own... Wherever you go in March you cannot escape the sound of hissing steam from locomotives and the distant clank of trucks, and after a time you forget the noise and are surprised when someone draws your attention to it.

I stood beside the controller in the tower; before him was a little map of the yard with red and green lights that twinkled as the running trucks passed over points. There was a crackling of atmospherics from the loudspeaker and a voice boomed out:

'Ready to take the strawberry run, Dick?'

'OK,' shouted the controller into his mouth-piece and, as he turned round, he saw the mystified look on my face. It was still winter almost and strawberries were a long way off.

'Strawberries?' I asked.

He laughed. 'Not real ones. You see we have nicknames for the regular loads that come in, and we always get a trainful of trucks about five each evening from the brickworks up Peterborough way. We call the bricks strawberries.'

As I left the tower the trucks of bricks were thundering down the incline, automatically being braked as they passed over the points, and then sliding away into the dusk where the waiting truck-men jump upon them as they pass and, sitting precariously on the long brake-handles, ride with them for a while braking the speed to prevent one truck from bumping too violently into its fellows in the bay.

I met an old friend in March, an old friend of many of us. I wonder how long it is since you have seen him? You may never see him again, and I shall always remember March for the pleasure it gave me in that meeting with the past.

I went into a cinema, there are two in the town, and I felt at once that something unexpected was going to happen. It was Saturday night, the place was packed, and although the lights were up and a drop-curtain covered with inartistic advertisements of local traders was the only thing to look at, the audience, especially those in the rows near the stage, were lustily helping out the amplified music of a gramophone record.

Provincial audiences may not be so eclectic as the more sophisticated assemblies that politely applaud London shows. They do not criticise their entertainment – they enjoy it on the principle that having paid to be entertained they are going to be entertained whether the film is good or bad. Any deficiency in the film they make up with their own enthusiasm.

This audience clapped everything. They clapped the newsreel; they thundered at a short comic strip; they alternately clapped and wiped their eyes at the principal film which concerned the lives of strangely unhuman men and women. But at the end of the film, before their eyes were dried, they rose to their feet and burst into such a cry of exultancy and approval that I feared for the roof. The tumult echoed all about me and must have been heard miles away. I crouched beneath the blast of voices and saw that the reason for their cries lay in a small notice which had just been flashed upon the screen. In a second I was back to my boyhood, sitting in a small cinema in Ebrington Street, Plymouth, and my voice had joined the general acclamation. The notice was a very simple one. It went straight to every heart in the place, including mine:

Episode Nine of the *Invisible Death-Ray*.
'Dynamite Between Decks.'
Last week we left Dick Fairbright struggling with the half-caste Lope Chica at the top of the mast of the *San Pedro*, which is conveying an illicit cargo of munitions to the rebels in Montelegrad...

I can guess what happened last week. Dick pursued the villainous Mexican up the mast and there was a struggle. What the struggle was about doesn't matter much. These film heroes and villains fight in the same instinctive, mute way that a dog leaps for a rabbit. The film ended, I am sure, at the tantalising moment when the Mexican hit Dick a treacherous blow with a belaying-pin and made him loose his grip on the mast.

I was right. The film opens, to an accompaniment of cheers, whistles and shouts, as Dick, spinning like a top, drops towards the sea. A spout of white foam, a flash of dirty teeth from the Mexican and the waves close over our hero's head. The proud ship *San Pedro* ploughs her way towards ill-fated Montelegrad where Professor Campbell, in his hacienda, surrounded by rebels, is being forced to hand over his invention, the invisible death-ray, to the rebel leader who is contemplating a worldwide empire. For a time I forget everything but Dick and the professor, and the Mexican. Dick is not drowned. Swimming under water he reaches the stern and climbs aboard. Stealthily he unfastens the professor's daughter, where she is tied to the mainmast in the glare of the sun. They tiptoe past the crew, sleeping the sleep of the cinematically drunk, to the hold where they make a raft... Everybody knows what he is going to do. He is going to make a bold bid to save Montelegrad by blowing up the ship. He sets a fuse, giving himself and the girl, who hampers his movements by clinging to his neck, five minutes to launch their raft. The audience stirs with apprehension. Oh, why did it have to happen? The ever-wakeful Lope Chica catches them as they struggle with the raft by the stern. The crew awake, throwing off their stupor with miraculous ease, and there we all are – for each one of us is now on board that powder mine – wasting time by talking, while that fuse burns nearer and nearer to the powder. The camera darts from the burning fuse to the group on deck, and back again.

Nearer, nearer – only half an inch to go before the big bang – and then – the film finishes, a rustle of appreciation goes up from the audience who will be able to come and see what happens next week, and a growl of discontentment from myself, for I shall miss it. Never shall I know what happened to Dick and the girl, and the *San Pedro*.

I walked out into the busy street, wondering if it would be foolish to make a special journey to March next week... The scene in the main street helps me to forget.

Saturday night! Gala night in March. Into the small town have come a jostling crowd, the streets are packed with a slow-moving, joking, flirting, healthy mob; labourers from the fen farms and hamlets, their good wives... in they come to forget the toil of the week, the farm-carts piled high with sugar-beet, the loneliness of hamlets, where rain is the only drinkable water supply, to seek colour, warmth and laughter.

They have come by car, by omnibus, by train, on cycles, in pony-carts, and walking... farmers' sons, red of face, their checked caps tipped at jaunty angles, girls with complexions that need little cosmetics, housewives bulging with parcels and good humour, and burly labourers, their hands grained with work and soil, and their hair rising rebelliously from the slavery of brilliantine.

From the lighted windows of the inns come the tinkle of pianos and the sound of songs – 'Lily of Laguna' and 'I Won't Dance,' for these people, loving the old so well, are not so narrow-minded that they scorn the new.

And they are not all so bent on pleasure that they have not an eye to a bargain. Crowds cluster round the stalls in the square by the town hall, listening to the ballyhoo of the hawkers, watching the butcher as he smacks his red and yellow carcasses with a familiarity the beasts would never have tolerated in life, smiling at the loud-mouthed humourists on the sweet stalls as they shout their wares and keep a smart eye on small boys whose acquisitive instincts are stronger than their ethics – and only when they think the price is fair do these people buy, for they have little money to spend and none to waste.

At half-past eleven I stood alone on the river bridge. The streets were almost deserted. The cinemas were closed, the shops dark and the inns silent. One by one the cars and cycles had departed. The last omnibus rumbled down the street, over the bridge and into the darkness.

In the square a few people remained, gossiping groups of stallholders who had just finished packing their unsold wares into their vans. Soon they were gone. The river reflected a feeble light from the star-smothered sky and a cold wind ruffled the dead grasses along its banks. A cat sat reflectively in the roadway, making up its mind to some feline purpose, and then disappeared into the shadows.

Above me the illuminated face of the clock in the tower of the town hall hung in the darkness like a genial moon and a silence settled over March, a silence broken now and then by the sibilant chatter of locomotives from the railway and marshalling yards that give so many March men employment and yet remain apart from its real life.

As I turned away a last car dashed over the bridge, the white column of the war memorial gleamed for a moment in the glare of its headlights and then March, the weekend Mecca of the fen-workers, slept as deeply as the rich encompassing fenlands.

CHAPTER 9

ALL THE WAY, PLEASE

The fare on a London General Omnibus from the Oxford Street corner of Tottenham Court Road to the end of the Number Twenty-four route at Hampstead is threepence. I know of no other journey so cheap and so interesting, and although at one time I travelled the route often and at those hours when the working crowds were packing the buses in their hurry to get to their homes, I never felt able to sit the whole while and read my evening paper. Those who travel much on buses, tubes and trains over the same journey, begin to develop a fine sense of their whereabouts at any moment during the journey, although their eyes have never left their papers. There must be some sense of combined sound, speed and time which enables a man infallibly to rise at the right moment and walk swaying down a tube compartment to step on to his correct platform, all the while reading the evening paper. To some degree I must have developed this sense. I could always feel when the bus passed certain points of the route and at those moments I would down my newspaper and let my eyes confirm my growing sense.

There is little opportunity for conversation on a bus. Even if there were, there would probably be as little of it as there is on our trains. We are not a talkative race, we are too self-conscious, and while we may long to ask questions ourselves of strangers, that does not stop us from privately condemning those who ask them of us. The result is that train travel, especially, becomes a book-guarded monotony which must be endured that we may earn the epithet 'reserved' from foreigners who mistake our absurd shyness for something much finer and less blameworthy. To sit in a tube compartment, surrounded by silent people, some reading, and most just staring blankly before them pretending to be unaware of each other's existence, is to be irresistibly, but not altogether unaccountably, reminded of cows. On buses this strangeness is less obtrusive. Conversation is wisely left to the conductor.

There was always a scramble for the Twenty-four. We would watch for it as it came up the Charing Cross Road, spy its number amidst the mass of traffic held up by the lights and then, as it came sailing across, run beside it along the pavement, jostling, elbowing and fighting in a friendly way to get a place by the step. Some of the more daring travellers would board it before it came to rest and – if the conductor were not about – get a seat, while we were still struggling in a silly way to get aboard and effectively blocking the way for those unhappy people who wanted to disembark and let us take their places. Intelligence is not the predominant quality of those London bus crowds, though individually, no doubt, they are all quite sane and rational. In this scramble umbrellas were often effective weapons; parcels, no matter what they contained, unless it was fish, were no help. Fish in a paper parcel had a magical effect. I once saw a man walk, like an immortal, through a milling crowd about a Twenty-four by the virtue of a pair of haddocks, whose tails flapped menacingly from the end of a parcel. Later I saw him sitting in a coveted seat at the front of the bus, quite alone.

That was my favourite seat, and if some day you want to spend threepence happily on that route, try to get the front seat on the top deck. It is the next best thing to actually driving the bus. You forget the people behind you and become one with the spirit of the route you travel and the crimson monster that carries you. Argosies, caravels and stately liners, dirty tramps and wallowing coasters have all had their praises told in poetry and literature. Someday someone will write of London's buses and people will wonder why it has not been done before. Kipling would have done it well. The modern motor car is probably content with obituaries for its poetry, but the omnibus – an ugly name for a lovely thing – should have genius to proclaim its joys.

Recently, having the time to spare, I waited for the Twenty-four with the intention of making the journey again. It was long since I had gone up Tottenham Court Road, northwards to Hampstead Heath, and I was eager to discover whether my sense of whereabouts had died from lack of exercise.

It was late in the afternoon and the streets shone wetly from a recent storm, the air was full of rich, unnameable smells. People packed around me at the stop. With some selfishness, and a great

103

deal of pushing, I got my coveted seat, which was important enough to me to excuse my conduct.

The bus started along the road which once led out to the Tottenham Court Manor House, which later became the Adam and Eve Inn, a happier fate than that which has overtaken some manor houses. Today the road has lost its rural character and as Harley Street is famous for doctors, Wardour Street for films, Great Portland Street for motor cars and Charing Cross Road for bookshops, Tottenham Court Road is the home of the furniture shops.

I knew when we were passing Heal's and Maple's, but my paper did not drop for me to eye their splendours. It dropped as we breasted a much smaller shop than either of these, a shop I can never pass without a loving glance.

It is small, wedged between two large buildings, and presents a dark, cool mouth to the hurry of the road. From its shadows comes the gleam of furniture that shines with age and in its long cavern I have often spent many hours pulling out the drawers of bureaus that once held the love-letters of ladies who wore patches and powder and bit the end of their quills over their spelling; rubbing the dust from the lacquer of occasional tables with a wet finger; fumbling with those nests of boxes that travellers brought back from the East to decorate the drawing-rooms of Berkeley Square. That little shop attracts me more than any of the opulent stores whose windows show to all the glories which adorn the homes of the rich.

Once I had bought a chair there. The dealer had sold it reluctantly, for it had been with him for a long time and he had come to love it. A few furniture dealers are like that. They hate to part with their treasures and they are capable of belittling, and even lying about the piece on which you have set your heart. They are to be preferred to those who would prevent your examining a piece by their torrent of words and laudatory gestures. It was a bishop's chair, with a wide, tall back and arms that were flanged to take the weight of elbows. The main struts, which were of elm, were worm-eaten, but the worms had not passed to the rails and seat, which were of a different wood. The dealer told me that they would never leave the elm, for worms do not spread into wood different from their own. They must remain in the wood of their birth. Over the seat was a cushion of delicate green brocade, marked with a pattern of hunting dogs and birds, which he had handled gently as I made my purchase. As I passed on the bus I thought of his look of reproach as the chair was carried from the shop to find a new home.

At Euston Road my paper fell again. It was pleasant to think that not far away were Euston, St Pancras and King's Cross Stations, and that if I were minded I could run down the stairs and hurry along the road to Euston Station and be seated in an express for the North. The people around me in the bus, clerks, typists, business men in bowlers and tired-looking women, never showed any sign that they were thinking this too. But they may well have been.

There was, as always, a busy stir of traffic at this crossways, and it was pleasant while we waited to watch the crowd moving in and out of the Warren Street Underground Station, and to smile at the studied leisureliness of the young lovers who waited there.

Warren Street Station must be a great meeting-place for lovers. At one time I had known by sight quite a number of the young men and women who waited each night. There was a young man with a slightly humped shoulder who always carried a rolled-up paper and, because of the length of his face, appeared to wear soft hats of absurd height of crown. He was always slightly agitated, nibbling the end of his paper, as he eyed the weaving stream of passengers pouring from the station. Once I missed two buses deliberately in the hope that, arriving later, I might see his sweetheart. But I never did. And there was the young girl with the face and figure of a goddess.

> *What winning graces! What majestic mien!*
> *She moves a goddess, and she looks a queen.*

I called her Helen and watched her many nights as she moved about on the pavement, not impatient, but seeming lost in a sweet reverie that took her far from the bustle of the world so close about her. She was as lovely as Argive Helen, and mine were not the only eyes that refreshed themselves on her beauty. I wondered who her lover might be and what godlike attributes he possessed to claim the right to her companionship – and one night I saw him; an old, long-haired man with stained clothes and the peering, querulous face of one who considers that life has dealt with him unfairly. The violin case which he carried probably housed the reason of his disappointment. She walked with her arm in his and her step was light with pride and joy, and I was glad that he was old and in need of her love. Afterwards I decided that I might have been jealous if he had been a young man... It was pleasant to sit in the front of the bus and pick out people from the mass and then to weave stories from the cut of their clothes, the expression on their faces and the way they looked into the shop windows.

Then we were into the Hampstead Road and running parallel with Regent's Park, from where, on fine summer evenings, if the wind was right, I had often heard the noise of the animals. The rough, sand-papery growl of the lions coming across the frittering rattle of traffic had sounded like a protest against captivity on an evening when all the world was entitled to freedom. There was no noise of animals this time. We rumbled along, the tyres making a gentle susurrus over the wet road and I put down my paper long before we got to the Carreras Building with its lotus-leaved columns, as I call them, though no doubt they have a much more technical name. I have never actually liked the building, but there is that about its style which always compels my attention. It is Egyptian and, as if to affirm its origins, two enormous black cats guard its main doorway, monster cats with staring eyes that neither wane nor wax with the rise and fall of the sun.

We went on, past Burke's statue and up Camden Town High Street to the five-ways by the Britannia public-house. The High Street is what all High Streets should be, a stretch of busy thoroughfare with shops and stores where you can buy anything from a fretwork outfit to a suite of furniture, clothe yourself, borrow books from tuppenny libraries and feed royally on fish and chips; and if you are wearied of civilian life there are the Army Offices with coloured posters of young men playing football, urging you to 'Join the Army and See the World.' If the only reason for joining the army was to be given an opportunity for sight-seeing, this would be a happy world.

At Camden Town a young man came aboard and took the seat across the way from me. In Weston-super-Mare his dress and appearance would have caused some comment, probably rude. Here, he passed almost unnoticed. He wore a dark green velvet jacket, dirty grey trousers, a yellow tie and a green shirt. His hair escaped in a dark fringe at the back of his low slouch hat, from under whose brim he peered short-sightedly at a book as the bus began its journey again. It was hard to imagine that some mother once loved him, or that wearing such crude colours he could ever write good poetry; but probably his mother did love him and his poetry was good but unappreciated.

Just beyond the five-ways the road rose to a hump and we crossed the Regent Canal, a flash of brown water, a barge nosing into a lock, and then it was gone and I was looking for a shop which had always puzzled me. Over the window, in large characters, runs the cryptic legend O.I.C., and underneath this the name Wallis. The intention is to call attention to the shop – Oh, I see, it's Wallis's. But I had never made up my mind whether Mr Wallis's initials were actually O.I.C. If they were, I had argued, then his very bad puns had some slight excuse; if not, then some suitable punishment should be arranged for him. And if they were his initials what did they represent? From time to time I had invented new Christian names for him, and the best combination was Oliphant Inigo Clarence Wallis. After we had passed the shop I realised that Mr Wallis's method of calling attention to his shop was so good that I did not even now know what he sold. Perhaps a few people get beyond his device to a contemplation of the wares he offers.

From Chalk Farm Road the bus swung away into Ferdinand Street where there was, as there always seemed to be, someone carrying a wicker basket towards a small building at the end of the street. There was, I guessed, a cat in the basket on its way to be mercifully released from this life at the Cats' Home.

Almost opposite the Home was a new building, a block of flats I had not seen before, decorated with pink and blue colour-wash, and looking like one of the cheaper sorts of wedding cakes. The Maiden Road with its second-hand shops, the tantalising glimpse of the open market stalls in Queen's Crescent, where the stallholders threaten and cajole you into purchases with the greatest good humour, the queue outside the cinema... I took them all in, for I never had been able to concentrate upon my paper along here. I had a glimpse of the inside of one of the bars and was reminded of Educated Evans, for it was between here and Camden Town that he had his haunts.

As though it sensed it was nearing the end of its run the bus quickened speed and sang over the wet stone sets, twisting in and out and swinging heavily around corners, until we were passing up Fleet Road where, deep below the tramlines, doomed to darkness runs the River Fleet, and then at the bottom of Pond Street the bus finished its run.

There is no pond there now. A fountain marks its site. It was the last of the string of ponds that reach across Hampstead Heath and from which the Fleet had birth. Hampstead Heath was only a minute away. Very soon I could have been away from houses and streets, and the steady turmoil of traffic to where gulls wheeled above the ponds and wild duck foraged among the water-weeds. The Bank Holiday Hampstead Heath scarcely touches the real Heath. It is an alien affair which flourishes for a few days in each year, and confines itself to a small area on the edge of the Heath. For the rest of the year the Heath is more countryside than many places in Devon and Sussex. Sheep crop its pastures, birds nest in its coppices, and squirrels haunt the tall trees, and to the countryman in London it is a revelation, while to the Londoner it is a haven. Here he can be alone and lie upon his back and watch the sky and imagine London a hundred miles away... I wondered if I should walk out as far as Ken Wood House. But I had no time to go on the Heath.

The bus I had come up on was turning to go back. If I sprinted I could just catch it.

CHAPTER 10

NORFOLK

You must go to Norfolk to see Norfolk. It is not to be passed through, like so many other counties, on the way to the Highlands or Cornwall. Beyond Norfolk there is nothing but the sea. You can stand on the promenade at Sheringham, listening to the growl of the waves over the flints on the beach and know that before you stretches a waste of water that acknowledges no land until the icy plateaux of the North Polar regions are reached.

Standing away from the main lines of communication, which have brought so many eyesores to England, Norfolk has preserved a rural, yeoman character which few other counties can equal and none excel. The oaks by the roadside, the numerous patches of heath and the sudden woods, all have an appearance of age and solidity which dwarf the efforts of civilising man, and intimidate the arrogant pylons that conduct electricity cables.

The richness of Norfolk lies, not so much in its famous Broads, nor in the saltings of the coast, or the splendours of Norwich, but in its woods and fields and in the small country towns with their red pantiled houses and quiet streets.

Its roads run, gently undulating, across the heaths and through the woods. Tall barrages of dark pines affront the skyline and the gleam of silver birches above the dying flame of bracken illumines a scene through which it is impossible to hurry since the beauty must be savoured slowly.

A crisp, frosty day greeted my entry into the county at Thetford, which must be an interesting town at the weekends.

It is becoming a residential quarter for commercial travellers and their families, so I was told by a local shopkeeper, who followed up the information with a story about a commercial traveller which was a little unkind, I thought, considering that commercial travellers' families were helping his business. If you have had much experience of the second-rate hotels which a great many commercial travellers have to frequent you find them a subject for sympathy rather than humour, and can only admire the way in which they extract service from boots, waiters and office-clerks who regard activity as a sin and politeness as a vice.

There were plenty of places which could have claimed my attention in Norfolk, birthplaces of famous men, the sites of old monasteries and unique architectural works – they were all set out in the guidebook with which I had armed myself and which I neglected to use. Most of the descriptions were about as inspiring and attractive as a Yorkshire pudding which has failed to rise. Of Earsham all it could say was:

> Earsham. (Pop. 581.) Pretty village in Waveney valley with
> Perp. church (Perp. font, piscina, hammerbeam chancel
> roof, glass, etc.) on site of ancient encampment. Earsham
> Hall, standing in finely timbered grounds, to north.

Well, there are hundreds of pretty villages with Perp. churches
containing the full complement of piscinas, sedilae, fonts and
etceteras. I must admit the etc. did raise my curiosity a little, but
I assuaged it by telling myself that the writer probably meant
that it also contained some fine fourteenth-century brasswork,
remains of old stoup and mur. painting on E. wall. I did not want
to see any of it. Some of the Pop. 581 might be interesting, but
they would have to be foregone. I was not going to Earsham or
any of the other places which no good tourist should miss. I was
not going to make a pilgrimage to Holy Walsingham, or wander
around Norwich getting a stiff neck, looking upwards at towers
and gargoyles; though I have a profound respect and admiration
for those who like to do these things.

I was going, I decided, to see two places. One was the small town
of Holt. I decided to go there because it sounded least interesting of
all from the guidebook, that is judging it by guidebook standards.
This is the description.

> Holt. (Pop. 2,429.) Market day – Friday. Neat little
> market town of ancient origin and modern appearance,
> commandingly situated on breezy hill-slope.

That was enough for me. 'Ancient origin and modern appearance'; the phrase was obscure and I hoped that the guidebook was glossing over some awful unconventionality. There was no mention of Per. windows and Dec. doorways, no Norman remains and dilapidated rood screens. The commanding situation and the apparently permanent breeze which blew along its hill-slope were worth investigating, I felt.

And the other place I had found not from the guidebook, but from an illustrated map given away by the manufacturers of a commodity without which we should indeed be poor mortals. I had seen the map in the hotel where I lunched and wished I had one like it. It was full of drawings of funny men and women, comic cows and gnarled trees, all depicting little scenes from the local history of towns and villages. It would have delighted Robert Louis Stevenson and appalled Ruskin. I was going to the scene of one of the most horrible and yet the happiest crimes in history, a crime which has shocked the inhabitants of nurseries for four centuries and delighted them at Christmas pantomimes for almost as long.

Near the village of Watton is Wayland Wood, the local people call it Wailing Wood, and this is the wood which is supposed to have been the scene of the tragic wanderings of the Babes in the Wood.

There is a tendency these days to regard a statement from anyone in long trousers that he was once a Boy Scout as ludicrous. Quite why, I cannot understand, though I have met two or three people who have been nursing this awful secret of their past in dread, lest anyone should discover it. The Boy Scout movement helped my generation to find the countryside and an open-air life. Young people today scorn any such organisation and are quite capable of finding these things for themselves – and a sorry mess they make of their discovery too, at times. Boy Scouts have at least the merit of never littering places with sandwich papers and orange wrappers, and if they occasionally break out into brass bands and church parades it is a convenient form of ostentation. All this leads to my own statement that I have been a Boy Scout, and I enjoyed being a Boy Scout. (I was keen enough to be indignant when candid friends insisted that my imitation of the cry of a curlew was nothing like the real thing. I was a member of a Curlew Patrol and each member was supposed to be able to utter his patrol call – just why was never made clear, as it was so much easier to summon other members with: 'Hi, Bill,' or 'Come on, Jimmy.') As an old Boy Scout I pride myself upon my sense of direction. Apparently my sense of direction must be as good as my imitation of the curlew's whistle. Within ten minutes of entering Wayland Wood I was lost, completely lost.

The afternoon had turned cold and grey, and there was a light mist blowing up. The sky had a sullen look as though it were about to resent my intrusion into the land of legend.

I entered the wood from the roadway through a gap in the hedge. I never saw the gap again. I followed first one path and then another. Somewhere in the heart of the wood, I had been told, there was the stump of the old oak tree under which the children had been found. There was nothing to identify it, yet I was sure that if I came across it, I should know it. A tree with such a history must, I felt, exert an influence, an arresting spell, upon the surrounding atmosphere which would wake anyone into an awareness of its presence.

The thin branches of the hazel thickets, which covered the ground between the stout oak trees, whipped at my face. I slipped once on the mossy track and brambles caught at the turn-ups of my trousers which were slowly filling with a fine collection of dead leaves and grass seeds. It was some time before I acknowledged to myself that I was never going to find the oak stump, and much longer before I realised that I was lost... In the end I sat down upon a fallen tree and resigned myself to my fate. I was lost.

Around me crowded the thickets and the tall brown skeletons of willow herb; a pheasant burst from cover and shot away with the noise and speed of a rocket, leaving my heart thumping with sudden fright. A rabbit appeared for a moment, eyed me quizzically, its nose wrinkling, and then deciding that I was an unpleasant character, made a bolt for its hole.

My pipe got clogged up in trying to clean it with a thin hazel twig, which broke off short, effectively blocking the stem and thus withdrawing from me the consolation of tobacco. I did not mind being lost so much, but I hated being lost and not able to smoke. To deny a man the solace of being able to suck at a pipe when he is not quite sure what to do, is almost to deny him the very means of thought.

I was lost. I said it to myself aloud and it did not make the fact any pleasanter. To cheer myself up I tried to imagine what the wood looked like in the spring and summer. Anemones would sprinkle it with shaking white at first, with pads of primroses pushing through the dead drift of leaves, and then as the primroses began to pass there would be a carpet of bluebells, a hyacinthine spread to fill the air with a faint perfume, tantalising and unforgettable. Perhaps among the bluebells would be early orchis and the pushing, lettuce-green hoods of the cuckoo-pint. Pheasants would be nesting, blackbirds would call from the coverts and... there would certainly be robins, the direct descendants of the pair which had covered the Babes. I was reminded that I was lost. I looked around. There were no robins, and I was in no mood to be given a blanket of leaves. The air was cold and I thought of a warm fire.

Luckily I was spared a death by leaves. From the pathway came the sound of dragging and scuffling. For a moment my mind was full of thoughts of murderous uncles and assassins. Then a man appeared carrying a bundle of ash poles. When I explained my plight he nodded with a smile that expressed his woodman's contempt for my misfortune, and he led me through the wood to a little clearing near the roadside.

From him I learned of the other, and more utilitarian, side of Wayland Wood. The clearing was covered with lengths of hazel, ash and other wood, and piles of split sticks.

'What do you do with all this?' I asked.

He soon told me, and as he spoke I was not long in recognising that he was a man who loved trees. To him a tree was a creation of character and soul. He spoke of the hazel woods of the county as a man might speak of old friends.

Wayland Wood is about seventy acres in size, and each year a 'fell' is cut. The acreage of a 'fell' varies according to the size of the wood, so that by cutting a different fell each year a strict rotation is observed, and by the time the end of the wood is reached the thickets have grown again where cutting first began and the wood can be cut through once more.

'In the old days,' he said, in his flat Norfolk dialect, 'when the Estate wanted more hurdles and thatching for corn stacks than it does today, all the wood was taken from here. We used to fell about ten acres every year. But some years we've had to fell and use the wood for little else than pea sticks.'

I could see that using hazel sways, as he called the hazel branches, for pea sticks was abhorrent to him.

'And are these pea sticks?' I questioned, pointing to the lengths of wood in the clearing.

'No,' he replied. 'Things are a bit better now. Some of the sways which are not straight will be used for pea sticks, some for screen hurdles and some for stakes. The thin, top end of the sway is cut off and used for making fish baskets at Yarmouth and other places. The thick bottom piece we call a broatch. The broatches are split, we call it riving. Not many men can rive broatches properly, it's an art. When the broatches have been riven the strips are used for binding down thatching on roofs and hayricks. But thatching is dying out these days and when it goes so will the art of riving. It's a pity – but there you are.'

And there we were, standing in the grey wood with tiny swirls of mist sweeping through the trees. His face was sad as he eyed the hazel sways and broatches and I felt suddenly sorry, too. To rive a broatch is as Saxon a phrase as any in our language and soon, it seems, it must sink into the limbo of libraries, to be mouthed only by antiquarians and book burrowing scholars.

To change the subject, I said: 'Do you believe the story of the Babes in the Wood?'

'Why not?' he said, almost shouting and completely forgetting his sorrow. 'Don't you believe it?' In his hand he flourished a keen-edged slasher knife, used for splitting the wood. I nodded my head, agreeing. Of course I did. And if you go to Wayland Wood and meet him, or anywhere near it and talk to the local people, don't even so much as hint that you do not believe the story of the Babes in the Wood.

As I went farther north towards Holt I passed plantations of young fir trees, looking as though they were only waiting for candles and presents to be hung upon them to complete their festive effect. Already the frost had spangled them with shimmering trappings. To complete the Christmas picture came the Norfolk turkeys, flocks of them, stalking about the fields like untidy old ladies, chattering among themselves and unmindful of their awful destiny.

Pantomime children, Christmas trees, turkeys, and a county which is typically English; long, rolling roads, bordered in places by dark green rhododendron bushes and sentinelled by tall pines; fields lying bare in the moonlight, and tiny byroads that lead away to unknown hamlets where men are still content to pass their leisure with a pipe and a glass, and the women are kindly and hard-working... this was the Norfolk that I saw.

When you go to Norfolk don't hurry for the Broads, but linger in the real Norfolk, the county of quiet woods, gorse-littered heaths and rich fields; walk along the salt marshes where the wild duck and gulls roost at night, and where the curlews whistle plaintively while the sheep move slowly through the mist, cropping at the fat grass; stay in the little towns, for Norfolk is a county of little towns, and talk with the men and women. If the county has definite character, so have the men and women, and perhaps you will be fortunate enough to discover such a man as I did.

He was a sailor, though not from any modern battleship. How old he was I did not enquire, for his bearded face and figure had the noble stamp of dignity and vitality which forbade such a question. Born in Norfolk, he had left it to serve his time in the navy when sails and bare feet and a penny a week for boys made Britain mistress of the seas.

Old George was a great talker. He stuffed me full of tales of pirate chasing in the China Seas, wild nights in Hangchow and wilder nights furling a top for gallant rounding the Horn, and sometimes I suspected that, like a good sailor, he was embellishing his stories for my benefit.

'Pirates!' His head tipped back and the remains of his beer were gone. 'I've seen 'em come over the side in the night and –' with an expressive movement of his hand across his throat the rest of the story was told.

Old George's sailing days were over long ago. Now he lives in the quiet town of Holt, come back to Norfolk to finish his days where he was born. He is a Norfolk man and proud of it, and a sailor who could boast that he was master of the foremast while he was hardly more than a boy. If you are interested in sailors, if you would like to hear a spirited defence of the British Navy and an impressive, slightly blasphemous, argument for sail against steam, I will give you a clue to find Old George.

Somewhere in one of the bars of the Holt inns he sits most nights. The inn you must find, but Old George you cannot fail to recognise. He might have served as the model for the bearded sailor who figures on the cartons of a very famous brand of cigarettes.

Old George was not the only interesting man I met in Holt. There was a young farmer who declared that he was up every morning at half past four and had for his breakfast nearly a pound of steak, and he had his own views as to how the steak should be cooked. Looking at him it was very easy to believe that his creed in life was early rising and plenty of meat, for he was large, fat, plump-cheeked and jolly; a contented meat-eater.

On the outskirts of Holt is a well-known public school. Staying at my hotel were several of the parents of boys at the school, who had come down for an end of term concert. Two boys came in to dine with their parents and, tucked away by the fireplace at my own table, I was given a very illuminating revelation of the attitude towards one another of modern day fathers and sons.

The two boys were fresh, eager beings with that look of cleanliness about them which belongs so essentially to the young and happy. The fathers were business men from the Midlands, well-dressed, assured, but somehow a little conscious of the fact that they were self-made men and had not been given the opportunities which they were only too glad to afford their sons. They were of a type which is vanishing, men of worth who had gone out to work at an age when today most boys are still sitting in class. They had been successful, but their success had given them little time to acquire a mythical thing which they occasionally longingly referred to as 'culture.'

One scrap of conversation went something like this:

Father: Well, son, are you going to come into the engineering works with me when you've finished your schooling?

Son: Engineering, sir?

F: Yes, son. There's plenty of money still in engineering.

S: I'd rather be something else. I don't feel I want to be an engineer.

F: What – for instance?

S: Well, an archaeologist or perhaps do research work.

F: There's little money in that. You want to have plenty of money, don't you?

S: Of course, sir. It does seem a pity that all the things I want to do won't make me much money. I was wondering, sir, if you would let me be an archaeologist and dig up Greek remains around the Mediterranean and subsidise me so that I didn't have to bother about money? A man of science, sir, ought not to have to worry about money and you would be doing posterity a great service in helping me...

A few minutes later the young man of science with such hazy monetary ideas had forgotten his career in a vigorous discussion of winter resorts and the best way of softening ski-boots.

Never once were any of the boys disrespectful or rude, yet never once did I hear them pretend to an opinion which they did not honestly hold for the sake of pleasing their parents. Their parents, remembering perhaps their own youth, seemed undecided whether to be proud or perplexed at the enigmas which were their own sons.

Of Holt itself I saw very little. All the time I was there a thick, icy mist was settled upon the land, dwarfing my range of vision to a radius of ten feet. I cannot even confirm that it is situated upon a hill-side, for in a mist it is difficult to tell when one is going up or down or along the level. I went for a walk in the morning, hoping that the mist would rise. It refused to move and reveal the splendours of Holt to me. In the mist I bumped into another parent from the hotel. We walked together for company, our breath hanging on the frosty air in great plumes, and the hoar from the dead grass hung a white fringe on to our trousers. Our eyes being denied their natural exercise by the cloaking fog, we talked more than we might usually have done, but of the many things we discussed and confessed I can only remember that at one point he informed me that it was his father who had invented the first gas-meter for houses and had sold his idea for a ridiculous sum, to see it make a fortune for other people. When the first meters were put into a row of houses as an experiment, the houses had to be insured for an enormous sum of money, because everyone was scared of the new idea and imagined that, at any moment, something might go wrong, and the whole block be blown into the air. I wish now that I had questioned him more closely about his father and the gas-meter, for I fancy I have missed a romance.

The fog was unkind to me for the rest of my stay and did not lift until I was on my way back to London. Unkind as it had been, it could not damp my enthusiasm for Norfolk, and I am convinced that when the rest of England has been overrun with wide main roads and ugly suburbs and housing estates, and when men and women wonder how they ever lived without cinema and motor car, Norfolk will still be Norfolk, essentially England, and men of Norfolk will be sitting in their bars and around their fireplaces telling apocryphal tales and scorning the hurry and febrile haste of the world – the last of the real English.

CHAPTER 11

CARAVAN ON THE COTSWOLDS

Whether you are a nominalist or a realist I can guess what the word Broadway means to you. Broadway – girls in top hats, carrying swagger sticks and doing a jerky dance across a Ziegfeld stage; electric signs across the facades of many-storied buildings, and the blare of popular songs. If you have only been inside a cinema four times you know all about it, though you may have wondered why you should have to know all about it since it is generally so infernally dull and stupid. 'The Broadway Melody' was a song which, by grace of some virtue and a great deal of publicity bellowed its way into the ears of thousands of listeners and it settled the meaning of the word 'Broadway' for most of us.

That is America's Broadway, or so the films would have us believe. The English Broadway is a very different place. It is a little village, nestling under the scarp of the Cotswolds, with its back to the hills and facing the broad vale of Evesham.

It has a long, wide main street, bordered by broad stretches of grass, running gently from the foot of the hills into the plain, a main street decorated by houses built of grey Cotswold stone, which is a mature yellow when it comes from the local quarries but takes that quiet, mellow grey tone as the air dries the moisture from it.

The houses are almost all beautiful and the wide grass verges that separate them from the road and the occasional trees make a setting which enhances that beauty. These houses have been built to last, built honestly and from the material at hand. Timbered cottages, the almost ecclesiastical Tudor dwellings, and the austere charm of the Georgian houses: they reflect the spirit of the master craftsman who made them and portray the ages in which they came into being. Here, in the Cotswolds, rests a village which has resisted the attacks of jerry builders with a resolution which is admirable, and it may well claim to be one of the most beautiful villages in England.

It is a glorious example of the creation of beauty from the things close at hand, grey stones that glow with a refulgence which comes from age, roofs that are covered, not by dark slates, but with thin flakes of Cotswold stone and softened by a patina of lichen and moss, and well-formed doorways that in summer are overhung by wistaria sprays that rival the spreading bounty of the yellow stone-crop and arabis.

I would not belittle the appeal of ecclesiastical architecture. One would be lethargic not to respond to the effort which has thrown up tall towers, outspanned flying buttresses and fashioned lofty naves, in order that man might have a fitting place to worship. For all that, I like domestic architecture better. The houses where people have lived, quarrelled, made love and passed through all the turbulence and joys of living stir me more than the places where they have solemnly worshipped.

I stood in Broadway and looked at the houses, and I could sense the pride the builders must have taken in their finished work, and the celebrations which marked the opening of a house. Today there is little house-warming done. Before the plaster has dried on the lathes, the furniture is in and the doors have slowly started upon their warping. If there is any celebration it probably takes the form of a cocktail party or a high tea and the house is forgotten in the congratulations passed upon its owner by his friends – the builders have passed away, to be remembered only by bills. In my pocket, as I looked at the noble houses of Broadway, was a letter from a friend in South America telling me that he had just had a cottage built near the coast at Montevideo. There, if not in England, the completion of a house is still a matter for jubilation among the workers. When the roof is completed it is the custom for the owner to give an asado to all the workmen. An asado consists of a lamb or ox roasted whole on a sort of grid placed sideways at an angle over a fire. The celebration takes place out of doors and, so he wrote, is one of the most typical of Uruguayan customs. There is singing, feasting and a great deal of laughter, and much more of sweet Maldonado wine to celebrate the birth of the house.

When I saw Broadway and the Cotswolds, there was so hard a frost that the ground was white with a covering which it would have been easy to mistake for snow. The dazzling white of the frost produced some astonishing effects in a district which is famous for its peculiar intensity of light.

The sky was a hard pearl grey that shaded away into a pale wash of blue, while the barren whiteness of the fields took the colour and reflected it over a landscape that was chequered by long stone walls and marked by dark plantations of firs and crests of distant woods. The thin strips of plantations and woods gave me a quite misleading impression of heavily-wooded country; actually the Cotswolds are largely open and bare, giving little shelter except in the valleys. I put up a hare from the long grass at the roadside and it was in sight for several minutes as it raced away across the bare fields.

I stopped on the roadway which leads up the twisting hill from the village of Stanway to the ridge of the Cotswold scarp, and looked back on what must be the most interesting view in England.

With the frost there was the slightest mist that hung above the fields in moving scarves and veils, swaying and changing shape in the breeze as though some invisible body moved within them. Out in the wide valley, divorced from the earth by mist, floated the hazy outlines of the hills of Bredon, Oxenton and Alderton. They had the appearance of enchanted, floating islands and in my imagination I peopled them with a host of fairy folk until the rattle of a train in the valley bearing a dark plume of smoke brought me back to earth. It was too cold to stand still and indulge in fairy fancies. The trees were laden with a white foliage of frost and in a fold of the hills a frozen pond glistened like polished ebony.

As I moved up the hill a strange company came downwards towards me. In front there was a horse and cart, piled high with a sorry collection of household goods, among which an old sewing machine was prominent. This cart was driven by a small and very dirty boy who, unmindful of the reins, was whittling a stick. Behind came another cart, a roughly covered caravan that might have started life as a baker's van. The reins of the caravan disappeared through the open doorway and there was no sign of the driver, though through the black square of the van doorway came the sound of a woman singing and the petulant crying of a child. After the caravan came a very stout lady wheeling a perambulator that needed tyres on two of its wheels and, instead of a baby, held a gramophone and a bundle done up in a red cloth.

As the procession passed me I saw that the hood of the perambulator, the crown of the black hat worn by the stout lady and the covering of the van, carried a thick coating of rime, and I wondered where these wanderers had quartered for the night. Probably, I decided, in the lee of some plantation, and they had been up and moving while the frost was still forming.

As I was wondering how these people made a living and endured the discomforts of an English winter in the open, there were footsteps on the road and a man came into sight. From his rough dress, the greasy knot at his throat and his unshaven face, and more especially by the two rabbits he carried in his hand, I guessed that he was a member of the gypsy troupe.

He saw me, smiled, and asked for a light. He had a careless, easy manner, as though he cared neither for approval nor rebuff. His life had taught him a calm indifference to the ways of the conventional world, and he was the possessor of a philosophy whose chief principle was tolerance.

He told me how they lived; making clothes-pegs with sticks from the hedges, binding them with thin strips cut from old cocoa tins picked up here and there, selling daffodils, blackberries, mushrooms and cress in the seasons and – though he would not directly admit it nor deny it because of the rabbits in his hand – hinting that there were other ways.

'There's pickin's here and there,' he said, 'and is it my fault if a rabbit sometimes puts its head through a looking-glass without a back?'

'Wouldn't you rather have a settled job and live in a house in some town?' I asked.

He was silent for a moment before he answered, as though he were carefully considering the question.

'That's something that isn't likely to happen, mister. If it should come along I'd take it like a shot, if it weren't for my wife.'

'What's the matter with her?'

'She wouldn't agree. Her family have been on the road for ever since they can remember. They don't like houses. I lived in a house once, until I became a showman. We travel with fairs sometimes now. No, she wouldn't live in a house. It would be the end of her.'

He spoke with conviction and nodding goodbye swung off down the hill. As he went his dog came down from the copse above the road and joined him. I could not help thinking that, if I had asked his wife the same question, she might have defended her love of the road with the excuse that her husband was unable to leave it because of the gypsy strain in his blood, though she would be quite willing to live in a house. He was not the first person I had met who had produced a perverse argument to disguise a perfectly good reason for following his own particular way of life.

Economically there is no reason why we should tolerate gypsies. They would rather beg than sell and prefer poaching to work. Few countrymen have a good word to say for them and in towns they scare any housewife who opens the door to them. They get from the community far more than they give. Yet, despite their obvious vagrancy, there are few people who would not feel that the countryside had lost an essential part of its character if there were no more gypsies, if they were spirited away from waste lots by the roadside to languish in and abuse the hygienic amenities of council houses. We should miss them at fairs, we should miss the dark-skinned lady who suddenly appears in drab February streets with a blazoning basket of wild daffodils to turn life into joy again, and we should miss the warm signal of their fires, sending up thin drifts of blue smoke on summer evenings, as the family sits around the black stew-pot. Perhaps George Borrow is to blame for this soft sentimentalising of the gypsies. Ethnologically, perhaps, they are the Peter Pans of the world, a race which has never grown up. Merry, mischievous children, sullen and generous by mood, content to wander and wishing only to be left alone – what does it matter if they are uneconomic units in a complex social order? There is too much insistence upon economics these days, and if the gypsies like to flout the maxims of Adam Smith and Professor Keynes – more power to their arms!

From Broadway I went through Stow-on-the-Wold to Bourton-on-the-Water. Bourton has been called the Venice of the Cotswolds, and Edinburgh has been called the Athens of the North, and if you only know Edinburgh then you can have a very poor idea of what Athens is like, and if you only know Athens your idea of Edinburgh would amuse any Scotchman. It is a lazy habit to label one place with the name of another and generally it constitutes an insult to the one and a libel on the other.

Through Bourton flows the pretty Windrush. It is the one river I know which has the quality of prettiness as Samuel Johnson defined it – 'Neat; elegant; pleasing without surprise or elevation.' It is a neat, elegant little river, flowing, when I saw it, demurely within its banks and indulging in no acrobatics over waterfalls.

Over the Windrush as it flows through the village are low, three-arched bridges of a soft grey stone. Wherever I went I could hear the soft sound of running water; to the ear there was nothing unmelodious, for the eye there was much that was unsightly.

As a race the English are content generally to admit that specialisation is a benefit to mankind. Each man to his job, is a creed that has grown in popularity since the war. But there is one business in which the English will not admit the wisdom of specialisation and in which they proclaim themselves, by their work, as incorrigible amateurs, and that is the craft of signwriting. No grocer thinks anyone can write the sign for his shop so well as he himself, nor any blacksmith, wireless agent, garage proprietor or newsagent. Of all the bunglers in this noble and universal craft, perhaps the honest folk, who hope to augment their slender living by purveying teas and refreshments to tourists, are the worst.

I have seen the word 'refreshment' done in so many different colours and in such a variety of bad lettering as would give a real signwriter the megrims for a month. Bourton, like other places, suffers from the amateur signwriter.

The signs, maybe, we shall learn to endure. There seems no reason, however, why an intelligent community should have to suffer such a monstrosity as the trench mortar which stands, or squats like an ugly toad, on the grass by the river at Bourton. I do not know who had it put there, or who had such offences placed in a thousand other public parks and greens. I do not care if the War Office did find the presentation to public bodies of guns and armaments captured during the war an easy way of disposing of a lot of old junk. But I do care when they are littered about the countryside and in places of pleasure and recreation to remind us in our more serene and peaceful moments that man's ultimate destiny and highest glory is to kill. I am not a pacifist, for the simple reason that if anyone kicks me I am quite unable to prevent myself from kicking back, and kicking harder if I can. I wish I were a pacifist. Evolution has denied me the exquisite pleasure of taking kicks with a sad smile. On the other hand, I am not a belligerent or a jingoist. I want to live at peace with my neighbour, as does every other sensible person, and I have no desire to provoke bad feeling or start a fight... yet there are moments when there is nothing I should love to do more than to invade the smug council chambers of those public authorities, at whose instigation our fresh greens and flowering parks have been fouled by the evidences of man's unregenerate wickedness, and deliver a whipping to every man and woman present.

From Bourton I walked up the river and over the hill to the villages of Upper and Lower Slaughter, which are all that Cotswold villages should be, except that they make no provision for the thirsty traveller. At one or other of the villages I had hoped to get lunch, or at least find an inn for a drink. There was no inn. One house had a sign hung out declaring lunches, and, after I had with difficulty made friends with a large dog which guarded the doorway, I pulled the doorbell and was answered by a half-witted boy who cocked his ear at the word 'lunch' as though I were uttering some heinous blasphemy. He then disappeared into the gloomy echoes of the house to reappear fifteen minutes later, when I and the dog were beginning to get impatient, to announce that the mistress did not want to buy anything today, thank you. Controlling myself I explained my request once more and waited another fifteen minutes, at the end of which time the boy appeared again and, uttering no word, shook his head at me sadly. I gathered that lunch was off and left the house, keeping a wary eye on the dog.

My thoughts, for I was tired and thirsty, were sufficiently sanguinary to prompt the suggestion that the name of Slaughter had been given to the villages by thirsty but disappointed Romans, digressing, in the hope of a drink, from the nearby Fosse Way. Finally, I bought from the village store some sweet biscuits, of a kind which I loathe I discovered after I opened the packet, and some small cheeses. I walked down the river, eating the biscuits on the principle that what I had paid for I ought to consume, and thereby spoiling my appetite for the cheeses which by themselves

I might have enjoyed. To finish the meal I had to get upon my stomach among the frost-bannered grasses and drink water from the Windrush, trying to forget that some villages upon rivers have primitive ideas about main drainage.

As I left the hills a westering sun was dipping in a dull, glowing ball to the top of a thin crest of spruces, throwing the fields into fiery light and the valleys into brown shadows, across which were traced the black lines of Cotswold walls, typical walls of flat stones that blaze with the purple and gold of ivy-leaved toad-flax and stone-crop in summertime.

Nowadays the Cotswolds have lost touch with the world, and lost little by it. Agriculture, it is true, still flourishes there, but history has left it severely alone for a long time. Once the Romans threw their roads across the undulating uplands and patrolled the long vistas with their cohorts, and soldiers from sunny Dalmatia probably cursed the climate at Stow-on-the-Wold where, as the rhyme has it, 'the wind blows cold'. The first time I was ever in Stow my bicycle developed a plethora of punctures in the back wheel. It was not a modern bicycle and I had to take off the chain-case and release the back wheel before I could get to work on the punctures. Into the midst of my grease and confusion and bad language, came a short-sighted tourist who tapped me on my shoulder and asked me, as I was forcing the sixth of six particularly intractable patches to stick, if I could direct him to a shop which sold picture postcards. It said a great deal for the humanising influence of environment, education and religion that I answered him politely.

After the Romans the hills were left alone for a while, until the mercers came with their packhorses carrying great panniers of staple and turned the military roads into great highways of commerce that are still marked by old pannier bridges, Pack-horse and Staplers Inns and in the name of Dunstable – the Down Staple town – which was at the junction of two important trade ways. The Cotswolds once sheltered the great woollen industry of England, and merchants grew wealthy enough to endow churches, and towns which are quiet backwaters were once noisy with looms and the bustle of trade. Now the Cotswold roads have gone back to their original pedestrian purpose.

G. K. Chesterton made the possibly libellous suggestion that:

> *Before the Roman rode to Rye or out to Severn strode,*
> *The rolling English drunkard made the rolling English*
> *road,*
> *A rolling road, a reeling road*
> *Which rambles round the Shire.*

And if ever you are in the vicinity of Bicester late on a Saturday evening you may be fortunate, or unfortunate (it depends upon your view of these things), enough to hear the old roads re-echoing to sounds that were common before the Romans came...

All that is now left to mark the passing of the great woollen industry are the sheep that still crop the hill-sides and the tombs and brasses of past merchants which fill the grey Cotswold churches...

The passing of fame and industry has been a happy process; it has not left the hills scarred or the towns depressed. Everywhere is a quiet reposeful beauty, a beauty that takes its birth from the grey stones and seems to impart to the men and women of the Cotswolds some of the steady spirit of the hills and gentle valleys.

CHAPTER 12

NO ORDINARY TOWN

If a complete stranger asked you to be kind enough to show him your town would you be able to give him an interesting day? Do you know as much as you should know about your own town?

You are probably saying to yourself: 'Of course I do. I haven't lived in the place for thirty-five years without learning all there is to know about it.' Then you are an exemplary exception. Most towns seem to be inhabited by complete strangers, so that if one asks for information of a man standing on a street corner there comes the usual reply: 'Sorry, but I'm a stranger, too.'

Visitors to towns get accustomed to this reception and, learning wisdom, usually arm themselves with a good guidebook or trust to their own native wit, both of which are generally incapable of supplying the irrelevant information which they want.

Very recently in a small town in the West of England I found myself in the same predicament. I wanted to know something about the town and from the three people I approached came the typical replies. 'Sorry, I'm a stranger, too.' 'It's been there as long as I can remember – that's all I know.' 'Mr Higgins, next door, would be able to tell you all about it, but he's away today. I never take much interest in these things myself.'

I walked along the main street wondering whether I should leave the town when coming towards me I saw a tall, thinnish man, soberly clad, with the face of a scholar. I know the men with faces of scholars in provincial towns. They almost invariably turn out to be corn-chandlers who have one interest in life and that the breeding of pigeons.

Impelled by a quite ungovernable impulse, I stopped him and said gently:

'Good day to you, sir, I wonder if it would be a breach of good manners if I were to ask you whether you could oblige me by telling me a little of the history of this town, and what the major preoccupations of its inhabitants might be, and whether, as a whole, they are happy or depressed, in work or unemployed?'

'Why, I'm—'

I stopped him with a gesture.

'I know what you are going to say, that you, too, are a stranger here, that perhaps the publican up the road might be able to tell me, if he were not away today, that—'

I stopped short as I saw that he was laughing.

'I'm afraid,' he said slowly, 'that you are quite wrong. I shall be only too happy to help you, in fact I wish more people would ask me to do the same for them.'

'You mean you know all about this town and will tell me about it?'

'I do. Follow me.'

And follow him I did. When we started, Dursley, for that was the name of the town, meant only a name on a map to me. When he had finished with me, and there were times when I wondered if I could politely escape from his tenacious enthusiasm, Dursley had taken shape and life.

He led me to the top of a hill overlooking the town and then turned to me and said, almost admonishingly:

'What is the connection between a field of teasels, billiard cloths and lawn mowers?'

'Why is a raven like a writing-desk?' I countered, and wondered what there was about me which merited the pitying smile he was bestowing upon me.

'A raven is not like a writing-desk,' he said curtly. 'That's all nonsense—'

'And so is this teasel, billiard cloth, lawn mower stuff—'

'It is not,' he replied. 'There is an answer.' He paused for a second or two and then went on: 'I suppose that you had never heard of Dursley and had to look it up on a map before you found that it was where it was?'

'Perhaps,' I admitted and added, to ameliorate his scorn; 'but my wife knew it was in Gloucestershire. She is very good at geography.'

He gave me a look which implied that my wife deserved a more intelligent husband, and then with an imperious flourish he waved his hand before him.

'There is Dursley below you, and there lies the answer to my riddle.'

The town lay before us, cupped in a great curve of the Cotswolds where they press out towards the Severn. The hills, covered with trees, patches of gorse and pastures, sloped steeply towards the grey town which lay somnolent beneath a faint haze of chimney smoke. That somnolence I was to learn was only a pretence.

'It looks very peaceful and sleepy,' I murmured admiringly, for I was beginning to dislike that withering little smile of contempt which he apparently kept in readiness for all the ignoramuses who have never heard of Dursley. As I spoke his dark brows contracted with a frown and I saw his tall figure tremble. Then he gained control of himself and replied with dignity: 'It is a town – not a bedroom. And it is no ordinary town. Please come with me.'

'But what about the riddle, the teasels—'

'Follow me.' The command was not to be disregarded.

I followed and we went into the town. We walked along the quiet streets and, as I saw a dog dozing in the roadway, I secretly decided that my adjectives 'sleepy and peaceful' were correct.

Suddenly he took me by the arm and led me through a small doorway of a building which looked like a convent. I was left in a panelled room while he disappeared and consulted, apparently, with someone deeper within the building. After a while he came back and I was conducted across a small yard and up a flight of wooden stairs into a large building to find myself confronted by a blaze of colour.

There were carpets everywhere; plain carpets, chequered carpets, patterned carpets, blue, red, green carpets and carpets of a mixture of every conceivable colour. They stood in rolls along the walls, they overflowed from shelves, they spread themselves along the floor until my eyes became confused with the chaos of colour and I began to think of transformation scenes in pantomimes. As if to complete the idea of a pantomime and fairyland there suddenly sprang from the earth beside me a wrinkled, short-statured, cheerful gnome who might have travelled from some subterranean recess of the neighbouring Cotswolds. Actually he was a Yorkshireman. He began to spread more carpets before me to exhibit the various designs and colours.

'This one,' he said, 'is very popular in the North of England.' I could believe it. 'And this one we sell a lot of in London, and this, and this, and this...' He was plucking down carpets from the shelves, working himself into a frenzy of enthusiasm over them.

'Dursley is famous for its reversible carpets and rugs – you should have known that. Any housewife knows that,' said a familiar voice.

'And we don't only sell them in England,' the Yorkshireman was saying. 'They go abroad, all over the world. Why, we've even sent orders to Mecca. Think of that, sending carpets to Mecca! Like sending coals to Newcastle, isn't it?'

I was taken to the workshops where girls operate the weaving-looms, and sing popular songs as they work. They were all as busy as bees, and making a pleasanter noise for, though there was no reason why it should be so, their singing harmonised with the mechanical rattle and bang of the shuttles as they flew to and fro across the looms. I cannot attempt to explain the process of weaving, and how a girl manipulates as many as fifty shuttles each carrying a different colour and works with them a pattern that for intricacy has the Maze at Hampton Court beaten. But if you want to know go to Dursley and visit the works and then you will understand and, like me, be unable to explain it to your friends. If you are interested in dyes you can spend a pleasant ten minutes about the dyeing vats which hold gallons of gorgeous dyes; that is, if you have no imperious conductor itching to snatch you away to sample the other delights of Dursley.

Outwardly Dursley appears to be no more than a pleasant Cotswold town with no particular interest in anything but its own leisurely everyday life and with no desire to impress the outside world. Actually it is a town of dynamic force and full of industry. Its factories and mills are so skilfully tucked away in the valley at the lower part of the town that they in no way spoil its charms or hint at their presence to those who pass along Dursley's street towards some other goal.

The normal population of the town is not much more than three thousand. Between seven in the morning and six o'clock at night the population is increased to more like seven thousand, for Dursley's industries absorb the resident population and many more. From as far away as Bristol, Gloucester and Stroud, and from the surrounding hamlets, workers stream into the town each morning on foot, by bicycle, car, bus, train and motor cycle, to fill their places at the benches, foundries, looms, dyeing vats and machines of the various factories. While I was there the actual number of unemployed men on the books at the Labour Exchange was sixteen! Is there any other town in England which can boast so few unemployed workers?

I was taken over an engineering works, so large that it runs its own private service of omnibuses between the workshops.

Here I saw being made petrol engines that would function in heating, lighting and water-pumping plants all over the world. In the packing shops, strewn with straw and cases, it stirred me, though it left the packers unmoved, to see labels affixed to cases bearing such names as Zanzibar, Los Angeles, Cape Town... Cream separators, teak-wood garden seats and automatic sheep-shears for Australia – there seemed to be no end to the variety of articles made in the factory.

One workshop was full of the hum of modern machinery, which stirs contentedly all day, needing only an occasional attention from a mechanic, and alive with the movement of men doing jobs which machinery cannot yet supplant. This workshop represented the apex of modern machine methods and reminded me of the fantasia of Charlie Chaplin's Modern Times, and yet across the way was another workshop, as though it were an exhibition piece placed in deliberate contrast to its fellow, where coopers were at work, fashioning by hand the tubs for milk-churns and making barrels with such skill that I could run my hand around the insides and not feel the joins of the individual slats of wood. The wood-workers were mostly elderly men and all of them had that wise kindness of face which seems to come to those who work much in wood. Wood, unlike steel, responds to the craftsman and gives its best when it is handled with love and respect. If you know how to handle wood, how much it helps in an understanding of men.

'Coopering,' said the man of Dursley, 'is one of our oldest existing crafts. There was a rope-walk in the town at one time, but that has gone.'

'And what,' I said, 'of the teasels and –'

'Follow me.'

And I was whisked off again; this time to a woollen mill lower down the valley. Yes, a woollen mill in the west of England. Have you never heard of west of England cloth? Have you never worn flannel trousers made from such cloth or a tailor-made coat and skirt? Perhaps you have and never realised it. I was surprised when I was told that the flannel suit I was wearing came from the west of England. Until then I had regarded Yorkshire as the mother of all cloth.

In the mill I found the answer to my cryptic friend's enigma. What is the connection between teasel heads, billiard cloths and lawn mowers?

Unlike most mills this one does its own spinning, weaving and dyeing and, as well as grey flannel and white flannel, it produces some of the best billiard cloths in the world. Yet without teasel heads the cloth would be poor stuff, for that fine dress which billiard cloth has which makes it smooth to the hand as you rub in one direction and rough in another, can only be obtained in one way – by the use of teasel heads.

I saw huge stalls of teasel heads waiting to be used. These are fitted up in racks which, as the cloth runs over rollers, are lowered on to it. The tiny teeth of the heads catch at the cloth and bring up a knap which lies in one direction. Once the knap has been brought up it is impossible to get rid of it, and there is no mechanical device for raising the knap which is more efficient than teasel heads. Surrounded by every other conceivable invention of genius to facilitate industry the teasels retain their place. Nature's tool which man cannot satisfactorily duplicate or substitute with one of his own making. Somewhere teasel-picking must be a lucrative employment in order to supply the mills, but just where they are picked or cultivated the man of Dursley could not tell me. It was his one deficiency and I believe he felt it.

Without the teasel where would the billiard cloth be? And the lawn mower? When the knap has been raised by the teasels it is not, of course, of a uniform height and it has to be cut to the fineness which you can see on your own billiard table. Literally the cloth is mowed to take off the excess length of knap and it was the cutting-machine through which the cloth passes in these mills that gave a Dursley man, many years ago, a brilliant idea. Maybe he was one of those gardeners by uxorial insistence rather than from his own free will, and hated having to get upon his knees and shear the front lawn with clippers that brought callouses to his hands and wicked thoughts to his mind. If cloth, he must have argued to himself, can be sheared of its knap, why can't a lawn be sheared of its excess growth of grass in the same way. He did not dream about it. He did something – that was to invent the first lawn mower. He took out a patent in 1832 and today you and I cut the lawn by virtue of his genius and in the same way, intrinsically, as the Dursley mills shear their billiard cloths of excess knap.

By the time I had seen all there was to see in Dursley, and it would need a book to do full justice to it (especially if one ventured upon an exposition of the apotheosis so vigorously maintained by many of the inhabitants that Shakespeare was a Dursley man), I understood the Dursley man's intolerance of people who have never heard of it or regard it as a sleepy Cotswold town.

Just why all these industries should have congregated about the town is not clear. Perhaps it was the pure water of the river that brought them, perhaps a score of other reasons. Anyway there it is, one of the most interesting towns in England; alive, working and happy, and its difficulties are not the usual ones of slums and unemployment. In Dursley the difficulty is to find a place to live. Homes are being built to house the workers so that they shall have no need to make fatiguing journeys before they begin work. When the seven thousand have become a resident as well as a working population there need be no fear that the new houses will have crowded the valley, for there is plenty of room for building and the inhabitants have enough love of their hills and heaths not to spoil them.

CHAPTER 13

BATH

Towns may be divided, if you care for that peculiar pleasure, into certain types. There are, of course, the towns we are born in, the towns we visit and leave as soon as possible never to return again, the towns we visit and return to as often as we can, the towns we work in, and the towns in which we would like to have been born.

Apart from Bath I know of no town which, for myself, I can promote to the last class. Had I any say in the circumstances of my birth, and had I been granted a prenatal knowledge of this country, I should have said politely, yet firmly: 'If it is all the same to everybody concerned I should like to be born in Bath.' But children are singularly at the mercy of their parent in these matters, and there must be many a noble town which has lost loyal citizens through the carelessness of parents.

When the time comes for me to sit irritably by the fireside and dream of long-past youth, my brightest memories will be of

Bath. Not that exciting things have happened to me there, but that exciting things might have happened to me there. There is a jingle which occasionally finds a home in public gardens and ends 'One is nearer God's heart in a garden than anywhere else on earth.' And in Bath one is nearer the eighteenth century than anywhere else on earth. The whole town is crowded with the ghosts of the eighteenth century, a time when there were more men of distinction in science, literature and the arts alive than ever there has been before or since. Sir William Herschel, who, before he was knighted and became famous as an astronomer, was the conductor of the band in the Bath Assembly Rooms, and he gave private lessons in music to supplement a meagre income. His rooms, one of his pupils has observed, even then resembled an astronomer's much more than a musician's, being heaped up with globes, maps, telescopes, reflectors, etc, under which his piano was hid, and the violoncello, like a discarded favourite, skulked away in one corner. Addison tells in one of his *Tatlers* how he was awakened in his lodgings there one morning by the shaking of the house and, on being implored by the landlady of the house next door, went up to interview a supposed madman in one of her rooms who was causing the commotion. He found a well-made man of 'great civility and good mien' practising ballet steps. Johnson and Boswell who stopped at the Pelican Inn, Horace Walpole, who was not very fond of the city, Ralph Allen and John Wood, Gainsborough, and Beau Nash, and a host of others whose spirits haunt the streets and crescents, they have all added to Bath's glories, but to Beau Nash more than any other does Bath owe so much.

To tell what Nash did for Bath would demand more space than I can command, and has already been told better than I could tell it. About Nash there have been many books written, some good and many bad. Oliver Goldsmith wrote his life, and Bath in every street and house commemorates it. Beau Nash raised Bath from a dirty, inconsiderable town to be the most fashionable resort in England and the haunt of beauty, genius and vice. Finally he instilled into the townspeople a public spirit and, because he was a man with an eye to business, did away with as much vice as was compatible with discretion.

The Beau was a gambler, a man of ability and invariably generous beyond his means. Bath is proud of him, yet Bath has need to be ashamed of the way she treated Nash in his old age when, reduced to comparative poverty, largely through his uncontrollable generosity, the corporation magnanimously granted him a pension of ten pounds a month! Ten pounds a month to the man who was primarily responsible for bringing thousands each year to the city and had, through his own personal energy and solicitation of funds, established the Royal Mineral Water Hospital, which receives poor persons from all parts of the country who might otherwise be denied the virtues of the city's waters.

Today his statue looks down upon the company in the Pump Room, who read their papers and sip their water. They are an interesting collection of human beings. If you like to fashion stories of a man's life from the way he shakes his paper out and from his dress, if the sight of old ladies decorously knitting and missing nothing that happens about them sets you wondering about their girlhood and romance – then the Pump Room will provide you with a happy hunting-ground for your Sherlock Holmes exercises.

The waters of spas are, I think, always disappointing. The first time I ever drank mineral waters at a spa was in Buxton. I had imagined a concoction of thick, sulphurous, acrid taste. In fact, I believed that it was largely the unpleasantness of a mineral water which accounted for its medicinal virtues. Medicine, my experience had taught, generally had to be unpleasant to do any good. Buxton disappointed me. The water was clear and tasted almost like any other water, yet with a faint difference that was hard to define. I liked it, but I was disappointed.

And I was disappointed with my first taste of Bath water. Buxton had failed me but I had a great confidence in Bath. I took the tumbler of water from a fresh-faced serving-girl – dressed like an Abigail of the eighteenth century – and, lifting it to my mouth, wrinkled my face into a wry expression in anticipation of its revolting taste. Again I was disappointed. It was to my untrained palate slightly brackish, but far from being unpleasant. The 'slightly brackish' taste I discovered later is grandiloquently referred to in official quarters as 'an almost imperceptible saline chalybeate taste.'

Bath, although you might not think so, from the conduct of the citizens in the streets and the assured, comfortable attitude of the town, is actually sitting on a volcano, and it says a great deal for the town that it not only continues to sit with great complacency where other towns might rock and tumble, but that it actually derives most of its affluence from the volcano. The volcano has not yet spouted ashes and lava, nor is there any crater where you can lean over and watch the labyrinthine bubblings of molten rock. A casual walk through Bath will not disclose its presence. I went as near to the volcano as it is possible to go. I was taken by a guide down the stairs from the Pump Room to the great Roman Bath and there, almost hidden by pieces of masonry and carvings, were two wooden doors which my guide opened with great reverence.

As the doors swung back a gust of hot steam broke forth and swept about me. I felt the guide's hand on my arm and I was led into a dark little cavern at the end of which was a steel rail. I stood with one hand on the rail and looked about. Below came a mysterious bubbling and spouting of steam and I could see jets and gouts of hot water shooting into sight from a crevice in the rocks which were stained a yellowy brown colour with the waters.

'This,' said the guide, 'is the nearest it is possible to get to the actual source of the spring from which Bath gets her famous water.'

'I don't know that I should want to get much nearer,' I said. 'I'm not used to taking a Turkish Bath with all my clothes on.'

'That's not so bad as wearing glasses,' the guide replied. 'I get people like that sometimes and the steam mists their glasses and they can't see anything, so they takes their glasses off and then they still can't see anything because of their bad sight. So I just let 'em stand there by the rail and get properly warm and listen to the bubbling, and they come away quite satisfied.'

I wondered if they would stand so happily by the rail if they realised actually what lay beneath their feet.

The spring which you see, or do not see, as you stand at the rail, comes up from a depth of more than five thousand feet, more than a mile below the surface, and the water is quite unlike the surface waters which come from ordinary springs. The water in ordinary springs comes from accumulations that have drained off the surface and, flowing underground into reservoirs or geological faults, eventually come to the surface as a spring. Such, for instance, are the springs which give birth to the Thames, and those at Cheddar. The waters at Bath come direct and virginal from the volcanic regions which everywhere lie beneath the earth's crust. In the depths the water does not exist as water, but in the form of oxygen and hydrogen which fuse into water as they ascend to the surface, and as they ascend there is dissolved into them all sorts of minerals and health-giving properties. Before these waters can rise to the surface there must exist a fracture in the earth's crust which communicates with the gasses in the volcanic inferno at the earth's core, and it is on the top of such a fracture that Bath contentedly sits.

It is a morbid thought to contemplate whether someday the volcano below Bath may change its mind about sending up water and deliver a charge of explosive gases and lava. It has behaved itself for centuries so I suppose there is no good reason why it should not go on behaving itself. Volcanoes have, no doubt, their own code of behaviour.

There are various myths to account for the discovery of the medicinal virtues of the Bath springs. The stories are picturesque and mostly untrue; that they are all concerned with the same person points to something more than a mere myth. This person was Bladud, the son of King Hudibras of Britain, and the father of King Lear. Bladud's son, Lear, has a greater posthumous fame than his father. I doubt, however, if Lear ever caused so much stir as Bladud did with his crazy notions about flying. Bladud and his leprosy and his cure at the springs in which his diseased swine had bathed and been cleaned, is a story every child knows. The swine of Bladud and those of Gadarene have an equal popularity amongst schoolteachers. Bladud was a man of restless invention. Bath he had made, but that was not enough. Not content with imitating his swine he wanted to imitate the birds and fly – and fly he did, not heeding the tragic fate of Icarus. He made himself a pair of wings and, trusting to them, with that true pioneer spirit and faith in their own invention, which characterised all the earlier aviators, he jumped from the top of the temple of Minerva at Bath and very naturally broke his neck and was mourned for by a sorrowing people who probably whispered to one another at the funeral: 'I told you so. I knew he'd break his neck. If we'd ever been intended to fly then Minerva would have given us wings at birth!' Bladud, Leonardo da Vinci, the Wright brothers… men of different ages, and all possessed of the same desire.

Whenever I go to Bath I always make my pilgrimage to the tip of Beechen Cliff. There is no greater joy than to look down upon the city through the still air of a bright morning. The last time I saw it was on a morning when there was just enough haze to enhance its beauty without blurring its outlines. Framed in the firs and beeches of the cliff-top it lay quietly in the valley-bottom surrounded by guardian hills, its grey-brown houses and streets spreading up the sides of a natural bowl, a city of incomparable grace and precision, the creation of orderly and beauty-loving minds. Over the city was a spirit of peace and dignity and, although I knew that down in the streets trams were passing to and fro, errand-boys were shouting, and there was all the busy stir of a weekday, where I stood there was little hint of the bustle. I saw only a city, washed with a pale gold tint, lying like the dream of some immortal architect in a forgotten hollow of the hills. Against the grey walls of the abbey the dark shadows of its flying buttresses struck a quiet note in the golden light, and even the railway in the foreground, and a bulking gasometer away to the left, shared the glory that hung in a bright halo over the city. Its beauty was heightened by the black and grey tree masses of the hills, the green of the curving river and the open spaces of the town. It had all the mystery of a dream city, a mystery of delight not terror.

And Bath has some mysteries. Everyone knows about its mineral waters and their healing powers; not everyone knows of the mystery of the Roman Bath, that great open pool, so closely surrounded by modern houses and streets, where noble Romans lounged and bathed.

In the great bath there lives, happy enough in their splendid isolation, a school of goldfish. They swim serenely through the yellow-green waters, uncaring of history or the tourists who tread the worn flags at the side of the pool. Yet once a year terror harries the goldfish, for flying over the rooftops of the surrounding buildings comes a pair of kingfishers. For two days they frequent the baths, taking their toll of the fish and turning the quiet cloisters and pool into a shambles. The grey stones and the green waters make a background for the flash of their bright plumage and the fish are stirred into unusual activity. When the two days are up the birds disappear and leave the fish in peace until another year brings the same, or another, pair of kingfishers.

That the kingfishers come from the nearby river is certain, but why do they come only for a few days each November, and why, having found a happy hunting-ground, do the birds not exhaust its riches? A heron would stay until there was not a fish left... are the kingfishers more prudent, or are they perhaps the reincarnation of two Romans, visiting the scene of their former pleasure once a year?

There are other mysteries in Bath. What is the secret of a Bath bun? Bath buns are made in other towns. Go into any Lyons' cafe and you will be served with quite a respectable imitation, but the real Bath bun, with the flavour which marks it from a hundred counterfeits, is found only in Bath. And why are Bath Olivers so popular in South Africa? I do not know the answer to these questions. In a way I am glad I do not, for there is nothing so fascinating as a mystery which obstinately remains a mystery.

To wander about the quiet streets, and the wide squares and crescents of Bath is to be taken out of this century and carried away to the days of stage coaches and sedan chairs. In Royal Crescent there still lingers the spirit of that period of pomp and dignity when patches and powder were fashionable and men wore rich clothes and were only reluctantly giving up the wearing of their swords.

If there are any finer examples of eighteenth-century domestic architecture than the Royal Crescent and the Circus in England I have yet to see them, and if there are any worse slums than some I have seen in Bath, then I do not want to see them.

Bath, however, is progressing; it is aware of its imperfections and eager to remedy them. It refuses to live in the past or rest upon its reputation. It is alive, modern and not content with old methods.

'Some people's idea of Bath,' said a shopkeeper to me, 'is that it is a glorified museum. They come here with their heads full of Beau Nash, Mr Pickwick, and the gay doings that were carried on at the Pump Room, and thinking that the streets are full of decrepit old ladies and gouty gentlemen. We're proud of our springs and our history, but we're just as proud of our industries. Perhaps you didn't know we had any? Let me tell you, this is a modern town. Our shops are modern and we've got one of the biggest cabinet-making factories in England here, and plasticine works, biscuit factory and quarries... and then there's the Pump Room. They've got treatment apparatus in there, so I'm told, that is the last word in modern things—'

'Have you ever tasted the waters?' I interrupted him to ask.

'If some of the old Romans could come back and see all those gadgets it would give 'em a shock,' he went on and forgot my question about tasting the waters. Somehow it was never answered, and he was not the only one to evade it. I found that there were more than a few people in Bath who had never tasted the waters of the spa, though there is a constantly running fountain in the street outside the Pump Rooms where it may be had free.

CHAPTER 14

THE OTHER OXFORD

The Oxford air is enervating and the long, willow-hung stretches of the Cher and the Thames on hot days makes energy seem out of place. But there is nothing to stop a man dreaming, and there have been more dreams composed to the idle song of the river at Oxford than perhaps in any other town in the world. And in later years those dreams are remembered. If you were a student, and are now an unimportant official, you are grateful for the importance which once was yours in Oxford, though it was only an importance that came to you from your landlady and the townsfolk. And if you were not a student and lived in the town you are grateful because you, at least, have had the distinction of living closely to a cultured, refined world, sharing in some way the life of the intellectual, living in a city which cherished first the mind, and next the body.

Between them the undergraduates and the townsfolk of Oxford present a most amusing study in picturesque and pathetic snobbery. From the colleges pour young men who, although they may be members of the October Club, and sing the 'Red Flag' outside the town hall on the night of election results, cannot repress within themselves a feeling of their superiority over the unfortunate tradesmen and workers of the town. From the University point of view there is only one attitude to be taken towards the town; it exists that the University may be fed, clothed, housed and occasionally entertained, and this attitude may be coloured by kindness, condescension or faint disgust. A great many of the townsmen seem to hold one of two views. Either they secretly wish they were members of the University, so that they might enjoy their sports and, less often, their studies, or they scorn the University and say they are very glad they are not part of it. The first form is common amongst the young men and older schoolboys of the town, and to heighten their desire they sedulously copy the University graduates in clothes, so far as they can, and cultivate an accent which surprises their mothers and fathers. It must be said to their credit, however, that they are very often taken to be undergraduates. The people who scorn the University are the rougher types who could never hope to be mistaken for undergraduates while their speech remains as it is, and a good many honest tradesmen who, making their livings from the trade they do with the University, object to the patrician manner adopted towards them by so many University people.

There is a considerable body, fortunately for the sanity of Oxford, to be found amongst the townsfolk and the University residents who realise that Oxford is not solely a university. Oxford is Oxford, a vast conglomerate, neither university nor county town. It is more perplexing than Petticoat Lane and sometimes a deal more interesting. Few people realise this. Those who visit the town are mostly interested in the University buildings or the boating, and those who live in the town are often handicapped by their own prejudices.

It is this other Oxford which has always interested me. It is a tantalising, undefinable, mocking thing, and the best way to come near to any understanding of it is to throw away your guidebook and wander without reference to town or University wherever your fancy takes you. Forget the city of dreaming spires and grey colleges set about green quadrangles on which starlings chitter at the rising of the sun and where students and tourists take up their chittering when the sun is well established in the sky; forget the weathering gargoyles and the brooding dons and professors who walk the streets, happy in the supposition that the sanctity of their abstractions is a shield against the vagaries of traffic, and concentrate for a while on the other side of Oxford where actions mean more than accents, and which may well be alive long after the Bodleian has crumbled into ruins.

Oxford is changing. If you find Gloucester Green you will see a wide square where motor coaches enter and depart upon journeys up and down England, and where long ranks of private cars are parked while their owners do business in the town. Once Gloucester Green had a greater glory than being a car park. It was a cattle market. Every Wednesday from the surrounding villages and towns droves of cattle come clumping through the streets, by the shadow of Worcester College wall and into their red-painted pens. Stallholders set up their wares around the market and there was an interminable confusion of cries; the bellowing of frightened bullocks, the bleating of stupefied sheep and the ballyhoo of blustering salesmen. Black men selling corn cures, apathetic men selling religious tracts, big farmers selling broken-winded horses… the market attracted rogue and honest man, and was a delight to schoolboys from the town. There was always a lot of laughter, and the squat building of the morgue which stood in the centre of the marketplace was never given a thought. Though once, on a hot afternoon, I saw the crowd part, and two men carried a stretcher into the place. A few minutes later a man stood upon a cart and swung a great bell to attract the crowd and then shouted across the silence:

'I would like to speak to Mrs James, please. We understand she is shopping somewhere in the market.'

I never saw Mrs James. I rather hoped that Mrs James had left the marketplace. It would have been a frightening blow to have been called out of the happy turmoil of the market into the morgue to look at the wet face of her boy who had slipped into the canal nearby…

The Oxford–Coventry canal comes very quietly into Oxford, hidden by the railway for a while and then gliding to rest past the lovely gardens of Worcester College, to be overlooked on one side by the rough plug of Oxford Castle and on the other by the austere eighteenth-century building which houses the offices of the canal company. Attached to this house, for it is more a house than an office building, is a tiny garden which rivals anything the colleges can show and yet hides its beauty behind grey walls and stacks of coal and gravel.

Life on the canal has not altered a great deal from those early days in the eighteenth century when the canal was first constructed. The bargees are more domesticated and less unruly, and there is now no need for the private police force which each canal company once maintained. These policemen were very necessary, not only to maintain order among the barge families who took feuds seriously, but also to keep an eye upon trespassers, who were inclined to experiment with the canals. These liberties took many forms, the chief being the persistent habit (of farmers close to the canal) of tapping the convenient supply to water their cattle and fill their duck ponds; and there were times when young boys, perhaps spurred by the tale of the little boy who once saved Holland from destruction by putting his hand into a gap in the dyke-wall, made holes in the canal embankment and then shirked the responsibility of stopping the flow of water.

It must have been a great day for Oxford when the first barge from Coventry came floating along the new canal behind its be-ribboned horse, carrying a load of coal, a strange black stone to many of the townsfolk. The barge was greeted in state by the mayor and corporation and heralded to the wharfside by the town band. When I visited the wharf there were no boats in.

'You didn't arrive early enough,' said the man who had come down from the canal office with me. 'They were here last night but they loaded up early and got away before nine almost.'

'Is that usual?'

He laughed and shook his head. 'No. Only there happens to be a fair at Banbury the day after tomorrow and, if there's one thing a canal family love, it's a fair. They'll do anything to make their visit to a town coincide with a fair. Today for instance, they'll be travelling hard to get there. If they were coming to Oxford from the other side of Banbury they would be quite capable of hanging about and wasting time not to pass and miss it. If there's a fair anywhere along the canal, you can be sure that there will always be half a dozen boats hitched up for the night there.'

'What happens to the canal-men when they get too old to manage the barges?'

'They don't usually. They just go on working all their lives. Some of them save up enough to help out their old-age pension, and then they look out for a little cottage somewhere near the canal. Quite a lot have done that and most of the cottages along the canal and by the locks are owned by canal people who either live in them now or are going to do so when they retire.'

'And what about the children – do they go to school?'

He smiled. 'They are supposed to go to school whenever they are stopping in a place where there is a school. You know what that means?'

'I can guess,' I said. What boy or girl would want to go to school after days of freedom on a barge, and as most of them become bargees or marry bargees, the formal education of a school is probably never missed. All they need to learn comes to them in their everyday life.

Oxford has given its name to more than the Oxford Movement or the University Press, as you may know every time you sit down to breakfast. Even if you do not know about Oxford marmalade you cannot walk about Oxford, especially by the railway station, and not be reminded of it. In the marmalade season, which lasts only a few months in each year when the Seville oranges arrive in England, the factory near the station is surrounded by a sweet, tanging odour of oranges. It fills the streets with its bitter-sweetness and is sometimes carried on the breeze far into the countryside, to surprise the cottagers.

Most of the work in the factory is done by girls. Most of the work in most factories these days seems to be done by girls and women. In this factory, however, there is an added reason for the employment of girls. The making of Oxford marmalade was first started by a woman in a tiny shop in the town, and it seems only right that its manufacture should be carried on by the same sex. The marmalade was supplied originally to the colleges, where it earned the onomatopoetic name of 'squish', and its popularity probably came from the unconscious sales efforts of students spreading its fame as they left the University. Today it goes all over the world.

As I walked around the storage-rooms I could not help noticing that the pots used for home markets were white with black lettering, but most of those sent abroad, and especially the ones for America, were coloured and decorated with sprays of flowers and other designs. Why should the colonies and America insist, as I am told they do, on these decorated pots when we at home are content with plain white ones? Here is another thing I learned about the marmalade. When you buy a pound pot of this marmalade, you don't buy a pound pot. The pots are referred to as 'ones' and, because they are all made by hand, no two are exactly alike or hold the same amount. In one you may get fourteen ounces to your pound and in another eighteen ounces. So the manufacturers carefully designate them as 'ones', not one-pound pots, and what you lose on the swings you often gain on the roundabouts.

Oxford delights in queer names. The Clarendon Press is in Jericho. That is the name given, just why I cannot imagine, to the district surrounding it. The walls of this Jericho are not falling down, nor likely to. It is a modest, working-class quarter which bears its oriental name with a red-brick complacency.

Then there is Mesopotamia. Part of the River Cherwell flows through Mesopotamia. This is no arid, desert stretch, but a delightful tract of trees and green walks where daffodils and primroses stud the grass in spring and courtly swans sail the waters. There is some reason for this name. Mesopotamia is the land between the Euphrates and the Tigris, and the Oxford Mesopotamia is a narrow strip of land between two arms of the Cherwell.

And not far from Mesopotamia is Parson's Pleasure. Oxford has shown a happy genius in the naming of her bathing places; Tumbling Bay, Long Bridges and Parson's Pleasure. The first two suggest what they are. Parson's Pleasure might be a tobacco or the name of a risque periodical. Actually it is the pleasantest of the three bathing places. The two others are on the Thames. Parson's Pleasure is on the Cherwell, and is frequented more by University people than any others, though it is open to anyone on the payment of a small fee. Parson's Pleasure is for men only. Mixed bathing is not allowed for the very good reason, if one were needed, that there is a tradition that no bathing costumes are worn. The tradition is a University one and characteristically takes no account of the fact that all punts and boats coming up the Cher must go through the bathing place. This means that any punt manned solely by women must stop at the rollers outside the bathing place. Here it is taken in charge by an attendant who punts it through the bathing place and delivers it to the owners on the other side of the bathing place, whence they have walked by a footpath that skirts the outside of the bathing enclosure. This is inconvenient but necessary. The trouble starts when the boats are returning, for then there is no attendant waiting to take the boat. The ladies are relied upon to remember the bathing place and to hitch their boat up and walk around and tell the attendant of the rollers to fetch it. Boating parties usually remember. Occasionally, however, there are times when, into the midst of the male paradise of Parson's Pleasure, where respected dons and fellows walk the green clad only in spectacles and a copy of Plato's *Socratic Discourses* and youths lie about in the sun with no cover but handkerchiefs over their faces, there comes a lone punt manned by some forgetful female.

If anyone still contends that man has not a good deal of the anthropoid in him he should witness such a scene. The dominant desire at such moments is to return to the trees for safety. The bathing boxes are few, and only the lucky ones find room in them during the mad scramble which follows the intrusion. Naked figures spring frantically into the rough cover of pollarded willows, others flatten themselves desperately behind tall tufts of grass, some imitate the armadillo and curl into inadequate balls, while a few with great presence of mind dive into the river and grant only their heads to the intruder. Some few lofty souls continue to read their books with grand imperturbability and mildly wonder, as they turn the pages, what all the fuss is about. Meanwhile, the unfortunate lady in the punt attempts to do the impossible, namely, to cover her eyes with her hands and negotiate her punt through the bathing place. The punt zigzags from side to side, ramming indignant bathers, shouts affront the summer air and a fine blush mantles all that is visible of the lady's face. The fiasco ends usually in the appearance of the attendant. There have been times when to restore peace to this Eden, the good lady has had to be expelled by a couple of swimmers getting behind her punt and pushing it before them. And still I do not know why it is called Parson's Pleasure.

Oxford has changed within the last fifty years. The town is acquiring a greater prominence and the University is now far from constituting its whole life. The colleges are being surrounded by a ring of ferro-concrete cinemas, office blocks and palatial garages. To the East industries are spreading, motor car works, press-steel factories and housing estates. Even the river is changing. Medley Weir is no more, and I expect the cannibal trout that once hung about the whirlpools below the weir have now gone to find other hunting grounds. Instead of swirling turbulently by the lock the river now flows quietly along, past the tall poplars and under the arched iron bridge which holds an oddity few other bridges can boast. The bridge at Medley was erected by public subscriptions, and to commemorate this fact there is placed, in the centre of its span, a plaque giving the date of its erection and an indication of the carelessness of the persons responsible for the casting of the plaque. The inscription states that the bridge was erected from 'public subsriptions.' I wonder how that 'c' came to be left out?

It was on Port Meadow, that wide stretch of river meadow that runs from Medley up the Thames as far as Godstow, with the Wytham heights to guard it on one side and the railway on the other, that I met the Professor. I called him the Professor to myself, for he did not offer his name, and there was something aloof and academical in his manner which forbade the urbanity of a formal enquiry.

He was standing on a raised part of the meadow watching the movements of a small herd of Shetland ponies. From under the brim of his felt hat a fringe of white hair escaped, and his face was folded and creased with loose skin that spoke of age. His eyes were young enough and he held himself very erect within his dark pepper-and-salt mixture suit.

I asked him if he knew whether the ponies had been quartered on the meadow by some circus.

'I am afraid I do not know,' he said, and the depth and mellowness of his voice did not amaze me, for it was such a voice as I imagined he would have. From Shetland ponies the conversation went, in the way conversation does, to changing Oxford.

'It has changed,' he admitted with a touch of sadness, 'but I will not be so dogmatic as to say that it has changed for the worse. The men who are up now are very different from my day. There is not so much money about. I suppose that is the result of democracy in part and discretion in general. The town itself has changed, too, all these ugly new buildings and the constant traffic through the streets... It is, indeed, different from the days of horse trams and carriages. I can remember the first pneumatic-tyred bicycle in Saint Giles... Even this mound we stand upon has changed. Only a few years ago it was a corporation dump – now look at it.'

I did. It was a green, flat-topped hill from which I could catch glimpses of the river through the willows. The meadow ran away in a great desert of green, stippled with the shadows of cattle and dying into the blue haze of the distant hills. In winter it is often flooded and provides fine skating, now it was blooming into colour again with buttercups and speedwells. Behind rose the grey towers and steeples of the city, none of them so old as the meadow which had always been common land for the grazing of the cattle belonging to the freemen of the city.

'There was a ditch,' the Professor went on, 'around the bottom of the dump – it's filled in now – from which I have taken some very fine specimens of *Gasterosteus aculeatus* and various *Hirudinea*... sticklebacks and leeches, that is,' he explained easily, and I began to wonder just who he was. For some time he talked about fish. He was not only interested in them academically. He caught fish and he told me about the pike by the mill at Wolvercote and the roach to be found in a stream near Binsey, and then, since he seemed so well-informed, I asked him if he could enlighten me about the names in Oxford.

'Why is the bathing place called Parson's Pleasure?' I asked.

'I am unable to answer that question,' he replied. 'It was so when I first came to Oxford many years ago. I was until my retirement a few years ago a college servant at Magdalen,' he added. And then, raising his hat, with the restrained gesture of a man of breeding, he walked away across the meadow, leaving me alone with the ponies and the murmur of the breeze from the river. I wondered, as I watched him go, whether he and his kind were perhaps the only people who got really at the heart of the true Oxford, who could hold the balance between Town and Gown and judge their merits impartially.

CHAPTER 15

OFF THE MAIN ROAD

The passion most people have for speed, that modern itch to go from one place to another so quickly that travelling demands all the concentration of a racing motorist, has saved Kent from disaster. Wide main roads have been flung across it to the sea. Yearly, thousands of cars tear across the county towards the coastal towns, and yearly thousands of men and women and children sit upon the beaches of Margate, Ramsgate and such towns, and gaze out to sea as though they resented the bar it has thrown across their wild speeding. Meanwhile Kent has begun to ignore this daily flow of traffic to and from the coast which does not touch the real county and only spoils the environs of the main roads.

Along any of the great roads that lead to the Kentish coast it is possible, after the outskirts of London have been left behind, to turn aside from the highway and in a few minutes find yourself in scenes of rural and unspoiled charm. At one moment you can, if your choice runs to that kind of pleasure, be sitting in the bright, tubular-furnitured confines of a modern roadhouse, and the next be ducking your head to avoid the centuries old, adze-marked beams of an inn that was serving drink long before the highway which sponsors the roadhouse existed. I have no doubt that the wooden furniture of these inns is often as uncomfortable as the geometrical absurdities of the roadhouse, but at least in the inn you can breathe without having the act recorded upon the arm of your chair. Wood, no matter what the modernists say, is a sensible, appropriate material for making furniture. Man has some feeling and respect for wood. Chromium plating needs neither man's affection nor his regard; it is completely satisfied with itself – and resents being sat upon.

Kent today is fighting to preserve its identity, and Kent knows how to fight. It has a heritage of struggle. In the thick forests of Anderida, which once covered the area now known as the Weald, the Britons played tag with the regiments of Claudius, and later made life so uncomfortable for the Danes that they were glad of the security of the Isle of Thanet. The Cinque Ports more than once gave men and ships to the navy when invasion was more a hard fact than a vague possibility. And Kent is still fighting to maintain its dignity, traditions, hospitality, beauties and humour.

I know few pleasures to equal the freedom of walking the downs along the old roads which lead to Canterbury. With a strong southerly wind blowing in from the channel and the cloud masses slipping across the sky like great Spanish galleons driven helplessly before a storm and with little of the marks of mankind to remind one of the present, it is not difficult to imagine the coloured company that once trooped along the old roads on their pilgrimage to the shrine at Canterbury. Below on the plain the trees and fields stand shrouded in a faint mist, and the pastures of the lower slopes change colour as the cloud shadows come and go, and in the valleys twist thin rivers, the haunt of heron, moorhen and otter.

It was in one of these valleys that I met with a typical example of Kentish humour. I was walking along the roadway by the river when, from ahead of me, I heard the sound of hammering. I came up with a labourer who was standing by a gateway. He turned as I stopped and I saw that he had just fixed to a tree a red and white notice, reading: BEWARE OF THE BULL.

I looked into the field. There was no bull there, though there were some bullocks cropping the grass.

'And when is the bull going to be put in the field?' I asked.

He hesitated before replying, and I was conscious that he was examining me critically. I must have passed muster, for he said:

'Der ain't goin' to be any bull.'

'Then why the notice?'

Again he hesitated, then he grinned broadly and shook his head. 'Well, it's like this. Der's a short cut across this li'l ole field to the road at the top. It's a public footpath, but master has got tired of folks from the town using it and forgetting to shut the gates after 'em, so that the li'l ole bullocks git out. I reckon this notice'll make 'em take the long way round in future!'

'Except those who know the difference between a bull and a bullock and realise that there's nothing to fear in the field.'

He laughed and, lifting his cap with one hand, scratched the top of his head. 'Folks that know that much ain't likely to leave gates open or trample down mowing-grass.'

His laughter followed me up the road, and I wondered how successful his dodge would be. Kent is like that – ready to welcome you if you treat it with respect, and readier to mislead you if you ignore its customs and affront good manners.

Every 'Beware of a Bull' sign in Kent is not, of course, a fake, and it is advisable to treat them all with respect. If people persist in leaving gates open, or climbing them away from the hinge end and weakening them, or breaking through hedges and letting their dogs run wild through game preserves – then they must expect the consequences. Farmers in all counties are long-suffering folk and wonderfully patient. When they do become bad-tempered it lasts and it is unpleasant for someone. After all, a farm is a factory. Who would dream of walking through the Morris-Cowley motor car works, tampering with the machinery, opening the doors of drying ovens, and occasionally kicking over a pile of mudguards? Then why do we not treat the farmers' factories with the same respect? Remember, if you leave a gate open and let a ram from one field get into another full of ewes, you may have been the innocent cause of enough trouble to make all the difference between a farmer's profit and loss for the year, and perhaps for many years to come.

The show places of Kent are easy to find. Canterbury and Reculver, Sandwich and Maidstone, Chilham Castle and Romney Marsh (and remember it is pronounced Rumney)... these do not hide themselves away. Their beauties are worthy of the interest of the thousands who visit them. Yet Kent has other, not so well known, places of simpler charm. This little-known Kent is off the main roads, tucked away in little valleys and folds of the downs. Here you may discover beauties amid isolation which you might have imagined the twentieth century had banished from the earth.

I know a hamlet, within ten miles of Canterbury, which is four miles from an omnibus route and farther from a station, which has no main drainage or electric lighting, where no newsboy considers it worth his while to carry a morning paper, where it is only with great difficulty that a grocer is persuaded to make weekly deliveries, and where, because the local farms do not keep dairy cattle, the residents have to drink goat's milk. This may sound terrible to you; actually, there are few finer spots in the whole of England, and from what I know of the people there they are healthy and happy despite the goat's milk and lack of a paper.

If you want to find such places you must leave the main roads – and often abandon your car. The next time you are in Kent and tired of the pleasures of Canterbury and the coast, try to find this valley where time is a loosely observed convention and life a neighbourly affair. I will give you some clues to it, but not many, for I am, with others, jealous of my secret and do not intend to provide too easy a guide to beauty which is worth hunting for.

The valley is reached by turning off the main road that runs between Ashford and Canterbury, and the turning is close to an old country house where Jane Austen once spent some time. The valley itself lies off the edge of the downs that curve away to the South Foreland and is almost in the Weald. The road that runs down into the valley is rough and rutted and just wide enough for a car, though even with the smallest car the hazel boughs beat at the mudguards and the blood-red leaves of the dogwood flick at the windows. Along the crest of the valley stands a dark fir wood, brightened by patches of beech and sycamore. Wood pigeons and hawks nest in the tall trees and woodpeckers skirt around it, their colours vying with the occasional flash of jays' wings. At evening the hawks come sailing down from the tall firs to quarter the rough pastures and from the depths of the wood the dog fox barks.

In spring the ground is covered with bluebells and windflowers, and young rabbits scuttle for safety from under the spreading wood sage. Across the mouth of the valley stands a row of tall elms, forming a break against the north wind. Along the other ridge of the valley runs a series of shaves, as the natives call the spinneys and copses.

The fields, in spring and summer, are a wilderness of flowers, tall mulleins, primroses, centaury, rock roses, early orchis, prim yellow-worts and ox-eyed daisies, and the air is filled with the scent of thyme and marjoram clumps. Even in winter the valley has a sad, barren beauty that lingers in the mind.

And, as though to complete the natural beauty of the valley, there stands in its midst a sixteenth-century farmhouse. Its cream walls and dark framework of beams face the hills as they were facing them when De Ruyter sailed up the Medway in 1667 to destroy the shipping at Chatham. Even then the craftsmen who fashioned the wide rooms and carved the open fireplaces and cut the date 1595 over the porch way, were probably all dead. Under the barge boards of the gables and about the diamond-paned windows, some of which still retain their original horn glass, fly sparrows and starlings, and owls hunt through the huge barns at night. By the side of the house, and spreading half over it, is an enormous walnut tree which was no more than a sapling when Catharine Carter, the first tenant and probable builder of the house, had her initials carved over the doorway.

Kate Carter must have been a remarkable woman. She was an old lady when she went there to live. She wanted to be alone and have a house of her own where she could be truly mistress. So she gave up being the unconsidered dowager in a wealthy family and built herself what came to be known as 'Kate's Folly.' And Kate's Folly stands today, though it carries a different name now, just as she built it, and it is said that at night in the large room in the front of the house, where the family crest is cut over the beam of the fireplace, she can be heard counting out her gold, piece by piece and sighing. Sighing, perhaps, that she was too old to enjoy the spending of it. Sighing, perhaps, because she was loved not for herself, but for her gold – sighing – who knows why?

Beyond the farmhouse there is no road up the valley, though against the hillside can be traced the mark of an old track. By the roadside on the hill above the valley is a dark church, hedged about by yews and beeches in which jackdaws and woodpeckers nest. It is a church which is far too large for the tiny village which it serves. If you go down into the village you will find good company at the *Man of Kent* and, maybe, get directions to find your way over into the valley and the old farmhouse. You may hear also the story of the beech which was blown over one stormy night outside the churchyard and of the skeleton which was found tangled in its roots.

The skeleton belonged to a murderer buried in unconsecrated ground outside the church. He had been the servant of the village rector, but his master's extreme meanness and cruelty had at last driven him to wild revenge. One night he murdered him and dropped his body down a well. Although I feel I should not, I cannot repress a certain sympathy for the murderer. If you find the village, please do not take any credence of the village sceptic's story that the skeleton was not that of a man but belonged to a sheep. There are always sceptics, even in the heart of Kent.

If you want to see the true Kent, find that valley. It will be difficult to find. The reward is worthy of the trouble. And even if you do not find the valley, in your wanderings you may come across another as beautiful.

CHAPTER 16

EXERCISE WITH A MAP

I was turning out an old cupboard when I came across the map. Turning out cupboards is a leisurely, fascinating occupation. I always carefully lock the room door before I begin, as I cannot bear to be interrupted in my pleasure. I never cease to be surprised at the odd collection which accumulates. Tattered exercise books come to light, containing cryptic notes which I puzzle over and have to give up. When the notes are in shorthand I am likely to become bad-tempered, for my style is not Pitman's so much as Canning's and is more an exercise in mnemonics than systematic shorthand. The map came to light from the heart of a bundle of old bills, a photograph of a litter of bull terrier pups and a catalogue of a past motor car show at Olympia whose pages were being used for the pressing of flowers. A stem of dried bugle, brown and crisp, fell from the catalogue and as I bent to retrieve it I saw the map. I forgot the bugle and took up the map.

It was an ordinary Ordnance Survey sheet. The covers were frayed and bent and the picture which had once graced the front cover had lost all its colour to a dark brown stain. I remembered that stain at once, and with the memory came a hundred others of a springtime when I had been able to forget work and all the cares which sit so heavily upon a young man who persists in taking himself seriously.

I stretched myself on the floor and smoothed the map out before me. Are there any colours in the world more vivid than the blue, green and browns of an Ordnance Survey map? The tortuous accuracy of contours, the black huddles which are towns and the grey markings that may mean anything from a gravel pit to a sand dune, the red and yellow wriggling of roads and the blue tracery of rivers... here is a language which goes right to the heart. It took me away from the room to the bar of an inn at Porlock on a hot, sunny morning. Flies were buzzing against the window-panes and through the open doorway came the dry smell of dust and the noise of passing traffic. A fat man leaned against the bar with a giant tankard of beer before him, a tankard so large that it made me feel ashamed of my modest glass.

'Going walking?' he asked, seeing the pack by my side. I nodded.

'Proper craze for that kind of thing these days. I had a couple of young fellows come to me the other night and ask if they could put up their tent in one of my fields. I told 'un that they were welcome to sleep in the barn if they liked. T'would have been more comfortable on the hay in there; but blame me if they didn't say they preferred to sleep in their tent. Some folks is funny.'

I gathered that he included me in this last category, but I did not mind. I was at peace with the world.

I took up my pack and with a nod to the farmer left the inn. Outside the air was full of life and colour. The fruit trees were in blossom and there was a heavy scent of may coming from some tree hidden in a garden. A cottage garden I passed was smothered by a glorious blaze of wallflowers, their rich, heavy scent burdening the air.

I left the town by a small footpath that ran alongside the church and struck away up a rutted lane towards Horner water. The hedges were thick with ivy and young leaf, and into the tiny runnel of water at the side of the road the stitch-wort was dropping its white petals. Going up Horner water I disturbed a hen from the bank and found a nest with two eggs in it. I wondered if the cottager knew of his hen's truancy and then took the eggs and left fourpence in the nest. If the money did not console the hen it would compensate the cottager if he were watching the nest. That was not the only nest I found in Horner. There was a wren's nest tucked away at the base of an oak tree. The bird sat determinedly on her eggs until I could have stroked her head. When she did fly off and let me see the eggs she kept up a constant scolding from the branches of the oak. I left the wren to her eggs and went on up the valley. The steep slopes were covered with oaks and the litter of dead bracken. Here and there were new fronds of bracken breaking through the brown earth, their tops curled over like the tips of shepherds' crooks.

On the map a footpath was shown leading up from the left of the valley, across Cloutsham Ball and on to Dunkery. I found the footpath and very quickly lost it. I did not care. All the day was mine and I could see the great dome of Dunkery hanging high in the sky before me.

I climbed out of the valley and into the dead bracken and heather. From the valley behind me a cuckoo called incessantly, and I met no one all the way to Dunkery except a schoolboy carrying a specimen-tin, who asked me the time. I told him, noted the faintly-concealed surprise on his face, and long afterwards, as I sat sucking my eggs on Dunkery and watching the silver glitter of the sea where the Bristol Channel lost itself in the haze about the Welsh coast, I discovered that my watch had stopped early that morning. For the rest of the walk it remained silent and still.

I do not know what there is about Exmoor that is more satisfying than Dartmoor. Perhaps it is that Exmoor is richer and has more life. The hills are gently rounded until they fall to the deep valleys and then the slopes are almost precipitous. Nowhere is the eye brought to rest with a jerk and everywhere it is pleased by a succession of royal and soothing colours, the brown sweep of dead bracken, the growing purple of the heather, the sheen of the sea beyond the hills and the yellow-green oak masses in the valleys.

Beneath the heather was the bright green of the whortleberries. Whortleberries are the walker's greatest enemy. In the autumn it is impossible, for me at least, to walk far; the temptation to lie down in a patch and laze away the hours looking at the sky while a hand moves over the shrubs picking off the berries and carrying them to a never-satisfied mouth is too strong. In Devon this sin can be indulged, though more rarely, when the wild strawberries are in fruit.

I was reluctant to leave Dunkery. I did not want to lose my feeling of exultancy, to pass from the region of the winds that came straight in from the sea, so that I could smell the salt in the air, and to give up my view... but I had to move on.

I found an old cart track and began the long dip down into Exford. On the way I put up a stag and two hinds. They were not very startled and bounded away for a time and then circled to windward of me and stood, their heads in the air, sniffing the wind and eyeing me curiously. Dartmoor has no wild life to compare with the red deer of Exmoor. That is Exmoor's glory, though some might consider it her shame, since the deer are preserved to be hunted. Whatever one's opinion of the ethics of hunting, it is useless to deny that the hunting of deer has so far prevented them from complete extermination in England. Yet I feel that the deer might equally well have been preserved by more humane methods. From a humanitarian point of view, hunting is a barbarous sport which can give enjoyment only to those people who wish to exercise those primitive instincts which were only excusable in our dim forefathers, since they had need to hunt in order to eat. Such desires should be repressed in a nation which likes to call itself civilised and has no need to hunt for food. It is logical, however, to assume that a certain amount of cruelty must always exist in the world to give force to virtue, and whatever one may say about civilised man, there is no denying the spiritual exhilaration which is roused in mankind by the moving pageantry of the hunt and the wild clamour of hounds. You may hate all blood sports, yet the sight of a pack in full cry across open country touches something too deep within one to be analysed, in the same way as the blare of trumpets and the steady rhythm of a marching regiment has surprised more than one pacifist into cheers. Until mankind has learned to be critically aware of its early social history and has gained the ability to control the predatory atavism which lies so near the surface of its stream of desires, we shall always have hunting and fighting.

Exford is a sleepy little village; it is not big enough to be called a town. Its whitewashed houses and hotels stand in the valley about the river. I had tea at the White Horse. The room was hung with Cecil Aldin drawings of hunting scenes and there was a smell of horses and riding boots to remind me that I was in the heart of the hunting country. The waiter who served me looked very sorry in his dress suit and was probably, I thought, longing to take it off and get out into the sun.

From Exford I took the road along the skirt of the moor to Simonsbath. Halfway along the road the map marked the Red Deer Hotel, and I planned to make a stop there and refresh myself before going on to Simonsbath. It was still hot and the road was uphill for a good way. I walked, thinking of the long cooling drink which should be mine at the Red Deer Hotel. The tantalising vision danced before me in the sun-motes and spurred me on. I was due for a disappointment. When I got to the hotel, I found only a dark-looking farmhouse, surrounded by a few beech and fir trees. There was no drink for me there of the kind I had imagined. I decided that a glass of water would be welcome, and knocked at the door. But it was a house of the dead. The sound of my knocking echoed hollowly through the house and suddenly, in the bright sunshine, I was afraid and my mind rioted with thoughts of plague and sunstroke, of farmers running amok and killing their children and wives. I left the house and got back on to the road again, telling myself that the family had probably gone into Taunton for the day.

I hurried on to the security and companionship of the inn at Simonsbath. The village lies right down in a dip of the hills, surrounded by trees and serenaded by the noise of the rushing Barle. All along the inland border of Exmoor the wild moor is fighting with man. In some places the fields reach up into the moor territory, and, more often, long peninsulas of the moor sweep down into the valleys, forbidding agriculture and defying man. At Simonsbath, there is a truce for a while and the woods and river make a peaceful haven where meadows spread their green and houses stand securely with their backs to the moor and their windows looking over the fields.

It was in the hotel bar at Simonsbath that I got the stain on my map. An almost toothless labourer was telling of the destructive, wanton habits of the deer, how they came from the moor at night and trampled down the peas in the gardens, spoiling what they could not eat. The night before I arrived a stag had got into his turnip field and had eaten a few turnips, and then gone systematically along some of the rows, catching the turnips by their long leaves and tossing them from the ground in play. The old man described this tossing motion.

'Ay, wicked as young boys, they be. A-tossin' and throwin' of the turnups over their 'eads-like this!' His head dipped and his arms flayed the air and my glass of beer was knocked over on to the map. The catastrophe stilled him and he looked at me sorrowfully.

'What a wicked sight. It doan't do to waste beer,' and he was trying to mop the stuff off the table and my map, but the stain would not be removed.

From Simonsbath I went up the valley of the Bade towards Challacombe. It was late now, the sun had dropped over the far edge of the moor and the sky was a pearl-grey. That valley, to me, seemed the loneliest and loveliest in England. It was wild, open and alive with the movement of birds. I walked on contentedly smoking and entirely alone. The only house I saw was at Hearlake, where a cottage fronted the road, and where a small girl held me to ransom for a penny, which had to be paid before she would open the gate across the road and let me through.

In the meadows by the river grew patches of marsh grass. Now and then a bat would come flittering from the sky to brush close to me and from the moor a corncrake called once and was silent. The mystery of the moor and the river closed in around me and I was filled with that trembling, delightful fear which comes to you when you are alone and far from houses and people. Had I been sensible, I should have turned back to Simonsbath and spent the night there. I kept on towards Challacombe, and before long I knew I should never reach it that night. I had walked a long way, the great gusts of fresh air were making me sleepy, my legs suddenly began to rebel and the pack on my back grew heavier with each step. The map showed no place to bed in before Challacombe, and I decided that I would sleep out.

It was a warm night, there would be no rain, and a tiny slip of a moon was coming up behind me. Once before I had slept out without cover. That had been between Salisbury and Bournemouth when I was cycling and found myself – through the grace of a hole in my pockets – without the money for a night's lodgings. It had been an unpleasant night, surprising me at three o'clock with a sharp frost against which the warmth of my bicycle lamp did not avail.

Now I decided to sleep out because I was tired and did not want to go any farther. I slept that night with my head in Somerset and my body in Devonshire, for the boundary line, I found from the map, ran across the ditch in the lee of the hedge which sheltered me.

I pulled long grasses and dead bracken and filled the ditch with a soft mass to sleep upon. I stuffed my pack with grass to make a pillow, took off my shoes and wrapped my feet in a sweater and then pulled my raincoat over me. I lay as comfortably as I might have done upon a feather bed. Away to the right was the road and between it and me was a small spring that flowed into a stream that meandered through a deep tree-lined cut towards Challacombe. I could hear the noise of the stream and the calling of peewits from the moor behind me. A spider crawled over my face and inspected my eyelids until I blew it away and, as I lay quietly on my bracken, a young rabbit came out into the moonlight and sat up as though it were imitating a Chinese Buddha. I fell asleep looking at the rabbit.

I woke what must have been three hours later, to find that my feet had come loose from the sweater, that my raincoat was covered with a thick dew and that the pillow had grown curiously hard. I wrapped my cold feet up and lay watching the moon through the trees. I watched it so long that the impression began to grow upon me that if I were rash enough to persist in my staring I should suddenly find myself flying through space, drawn towards the moon by its attraction. I turned my eyes away quickly and congratulated myself upon my lucky escape. Three or four times since I have had that feeling when looking at the moon. I know it is imagination, of course, but the conviction is strong enough to force me to turn my eyes away.

The growing cold that night soon took my thoughts from the moon. The cold started with my feet and worked along my body. I burrowed into the bracken and slept for a while. The cold did not leave me alone for the rest of the night. I slept fitfully, cursing my folly. I took the grass from my pack and strapped my feet into it for warmth, and I used the sweater as a pillow. I twisted and turned. The cold persisted.

I got up before the sun that morning and stumbled to the stream. The water was like ice. I forced myself to wash in it, gasping and panting for breath as the icy douche touched my skin. I ran around the moor in circles to get warm, and when my face was red and the blood biting through my body once more, I sat down and ate chocolate and two stale sandwiches and watched the sun come up. She crept very unwillingly into the sky and before she was high enough to give any warmth I was on the road to Challacombe.

I passed through it as though it were a village of the dead. There was no one about. Not a hen crowed nor a dog barked, and I felt myself inexpressibly elated at my earliness. While others slept I was on the road, enjoying myself. I was warm by now and surprised to discover that my night had refreshed me.

There is nothing in this world which gives a feeling of superiority more than getting up in the morning before the rest of the world, and there is nothing more annoying than to rise early and be met by the scoffing remark of a friend that he has been up for hours. Friendships have to be firm to withstand the irritation of such remarks as: 'What? Only just got up? I've been up hours.' Or 'Lovely now? Yes, but you should have been up at six this morning. It was grand.' Or 'Just because you've got up early for once, must you let everybody know about it?'

Of course, you must let everybody know about it. I had been up before birdsong, before the earliest bird, and I longed to tell someone about it. I met no one until I reached the crossroads at Blackmore Gate. There I fell in with a young man who had been up before I had. He was motor cycling to Berrynarbor to see his sweetheart and had been up since three o'clock. Just why he did not say. It may have been that he had come a great distance, or his impatience to be with his love had not let him lie abed. His machine had broken down at Blackmore Gate and he had started out to walk the rest of the way to Berrynarbor. He was resting on a gateway along the road to Combe Martin when I caught him up and we kept company the rest of the way to Combe Martin, where he left me. I was not sorry when he left me, for his idea of good conversation was to regale me with the details of all the road accidents he had ever seen and to mark the various twists and turns of the roadway with stories of crashes which had taken place. If his stories were to be believed the road between Combe Martin and Blackmore Gate must be the most dangerous in the world, travelled by a fine collection of maniacs. I thought of him later during the day and wondered if he and his sweetheart were sitting on the cliffs beyond Berrynarbor, looking out to sea and, as they held hands, telling one another of the accidents which they had seen since last they met.

Combe Martin must have the longest main street of any village. It is nearly two miles long and its characteristic features are the boards outside almost every house proclaiming that the price of Bed and Breakfast is four shillings and sixpence. In some establishments, I noticed, the price was higher. In none did it sink below four shillings and sixpence, and I wondered if the people of Combe Martin had met in solemn conference and decided on this minimum charge. Someday, I thought, a daring landlady would offer Bed and Breakfast at a lower price and then the village would turn upon her and refuse to serve her with food or accord her the amenities of life until she was forced to raise her price to their minimum.

I walked the hot length of street resisting the signs of breakfast, for I was determined to eat within sight of the sea. I did; through the open doorway I perceived the legs of the passers-by and the rocks and blue of the sea. I took a long while over my breakfast; I felt I had that much time in hand.

At Combe Martin I decided it was time to turn back towards Porlock. The map showed a footpath leading along the coast to the road that curves around to Trentishoe. I could tell by the look of it on the map that I should lose it, and lose it I did somewhere near the top of the Great Hangman, where the cliffs run out to Blackstone Point. It was a hard climb to the Hangman, with the sea and the gulls on one hand and the great sweep of country running away from the other until it met the pale sky miles away. The heat came off the rocks in shimmering waves and, as I clambered over a scree of loose stone on my way down the steep side of Sherrycombe, an adder slithered away before me, leaving a moment of coldness behind. The sides of Sherrycombe are composed in most places of loose drifts of stone and to descend to the small beck at the bottom of the combe is to walk with the mutter of tiny avalanches all around one. I had to empty my shoes of grit at the bottom and again at the top… The rest of that day is a brilliant memory; Hunter's Inn, when I was dying of thirst, lunch by a tiny stream with a pair of yellow wagtails to keep me company, and tea at an hotel in Woody Bay, where an immaculately dressed serving-man eyed my unshaven face and crumpled clothes with cold wonder, which did not disappear even when I proved able to pay my score. My consumption of jam and cream must have caused him consternation.

I returned that night to the comforts of civilisation at a farmhouse standing on the hill high above Watersmeet. A shave and a hot bath took the day's fatigue from me. From the farm the land fell away into the deep wooded valley that stretched back to Lynton and, above Watersmeet, divided into two arms, one running up to Brendon and the other towards Cheriton. The air was so clear that I could make out the cars moving up and down the shoulder of Countisbury across the valley. The trees were a greenish blue in the evening light where the shadows massed in the valley.

Before lunchtime the next day I was moving across Brendon Common, setting a course by the sun and doubting my accuracy every fifteen minutes, for the Doone Valley. If you enter the Doone

Valley by way of Brendon it loses most of its surprise and wild splendour. The proper way – at least I shall always think so because that is how I saw it first – is to come down Hoccombe Combe, across the springy turf, taking drinks now and then from the pools along the tiny stream where the boulders are covered with a soft feathery moss. At the head of Doone Valley, before reaching Badgworthy Water, there stands a ruined house, said to have been the home of the Doones. It was near this ruin that I found the skull of a deer. At least I have always maintained, against the opinion of all my friends, that it is a deer's skull and not a sheep's. I packed the skull in my sweater for safety while I walked, and I treasured it for years. At last it was lost, but I do know it was a deer's skull – not a sheep's.

I crossed Badgworthy Water, jumping from one stone to another. The water slide up which Jan Ridd worked his way catching loaches does not exist, and the Doone Valley, although it is remote enough, is not so inaccessible, nor ever could have been so hidden, as Blackmore made it. It was the ferocity of the Doones that secured them from interference rather than the difficulty of finding their little valley.

I did not go down to Oare. I struck away across the moor and dipped to the valley at Robber's Bridge and then climbed through an oak wood on to the main Porlock-Lynton road, and that night I was many miles from Exmoor.

I have been back to Exmoor since then. I have made my pilgrimage to the church at Oare, seen the window through which Carver Doone shot Lorna Doone, and signed my name in the register. I have stopped at Exford again and made friends with the waiter who looked so hot in his formal clothes, and I have even found the spot where I slept so uncomfortably under the hedge and, as I looked at it, wondered what magic there was in that blue evening to make me welcome such discomfort. But I can never forget my first acquaintance with this country, the momentary unreality of wild deer, the potency of cider drunken at midday, the long rolling sweeps of purple and brown moor with the solitary scrawl of a twisted may tree to break the line of hills, and the music of swift streams boiling and threshing over the boulders in their beds and flinging up spray to wet the low branches of birches... I sat for a long time by the cupboard with the map in my hand. Those three hot, walking days over Exmoor were a long way behind me. I put the map down. Perhaps it was all a dream and had never happened outside my mind. My arm touched an unsteady pile of books and they fell flapping to the ground. By the wall behind them something white showed, and from the gloom two sightless eye sockets fixed me with a sad stare and a mouth full of white tusks grinned at me. It was my old deer skull, the cranium covered with a fine mantle of webs and dust.

CHAPTER 17

DORCHESTER

There are some questions which do not need an answer. How long has Dorchester been a town, is one of them. Nobody knows, and nobody cares. It is enough that Dorchester exists without questioning its origin.

I know – and you will know too, if you have ever been to Dorchester – that its old British name was Dwrinwyr, meaning the settlement by the dwyr, the dark waters of the Frome, that its Roman name was Durnovaria, a prettier name, I think, than the other, and that in time it became Dorchester. Even when you know these things, you still know very little about Dorchester except that at various periods it has been inhabited by Britons, Romans and now the English.

I visited the town with a friend of an enquiring nature. His eagerness for knowledge is remarkable and his capacity to obtain it by his own research negligible. If he reads this he will not be offended, for he covers his laziness with the plea that it is better to learn from the lips of others than by reading from books.

We stood outside the Antelope Hotel and I said to him: 'Would you care to go to the pictures?'

'Why?'

'I thought you might like entertainment.'

'I came here to see Dorchester, not the films, and I want instruction. You've studied the guidebook, haven't you?'

'In a way. I've looked at most of the pictures.'

'You've been lazy. Well, you'll have to lead me to the various places of interest and read about them from the guidebook. Where shall we go first?'

'There is a picture of Maumbury Rings which looks interesting.'

'That will do.'

We found Maumbury Rings on the south side of the town. It is a wide, grass-grown amphitheatre, constructed by the Romans during their occupation of the town. Here they had their games and sports.

The town presses closely about this Dorset coliseum; a railway line hems it on one side, a police station on another and a road studded with Belisha beacons on a third. Despite these crowding signs of a later age, the old arena still retains its dignity and grandeur. From its ramparts we had a good view of the town, a spread of red-brick and grey houses, mixed up with the dark crests of trees. In the foreground were the railway station and the bulk of a brewery. Beyond the brewery, and less intimidating, rose the steeples of various churches.

'I notice,' said my friend, after I had finished reading about the Roman amphitheatre, 'that the grass of the arena is very much worn in places.'

'I suspect the small boys of the town. This maybe, is one way they get their own back on the Romans who bother them during lessons. They come here and play cricket. The glory of Rome has gone when small boys play ball where gladiators fought and died.'

'If I know anything about boys,' came the reply, 'they probably played ball in the arena when the Romans were here and kept a sharp lookout for angry gladiators instead of policemen. Tell me, did the townspeople never use this place after the Romans for their own sports and festivals?'

'Undoubtedly. I think the most popular form of entertainment held here were the Hanging Fairs. Public executions drew huge crowds. In 1705 as many as ten thousand spectators assembled here to watch the strangling and burning of a woman for the murder of her husband, a Dorchester tradesman. Her name was Mary Channing –'

'A relation of yours?'

'There is no h in my name,' I replied haughtily.

'A pity. They certainly had a pretty taste in entertainment. I think the burning after the strangling was rather unnecessary. I wonder what kind of man the official strangler was. It's diverting to imagine that perhaps he was a meek man, fond of his children and with no more ambition than to grow prize cabbages. I suppose he did it with his hands?'

'Did what?' I was watching the movements of a pair of gulls of the arena.

'The strangling.'

'The guidebook says nothing about that.'

'Would you go to watch public executions if they happened today?'

'I might go to one, but I certainly should not make a habit of it. Nor would many people, I think.'

'You're wrong. We haven't changed a great deal from those days. If men and women were hanged in public there would always be a crowd, and a nucleus of regular spectators who never missed a hanging. There must be something satisfying to watch someone losing life while you still retain it.'

'It sounds beastly to me.'

'It is – but bestiality is good box office. The smell of carrion is enough to bring the vultures. Have you ever seen a crowd outside the gates of a gaol waiting to read the notice that some poor devil has been duly hanged and sent to his Maker? It affords very unpleasant material for speculation on the animal antecedents of mankind. They can't see anything, they can't hear anything; but there they are, waiting in a crowd, just waiting.'

We left Maumbury and went on to Poundbury, a vast, oblong entrenchment outside the town and not far from the Artillery Barracks. Older than Maumbury, Poundbury's origin is lost in the dimness of the past. Successive civilisations and races have used it, but the people who first raised its ramparts and dug its trenches might have never lived for the little we know about them.

We walked around the top of the entrenchment, the wind from the valley of the Frome whistling by our ears. A hare started away from the round barrow in the centre of the camp and disappeared behind the rifle range by the river. The river was running in spate and the meadows were cut and quartered by long arms of flood water. Behind us lay the town, clinging to the hill above the river, solid, respectable and secure, its grey streets filled with the noise of country traffic, clerks working in offices, boys bent over their desks, shopkeepers making up their accounts and arranging their windows... all busy in a life which was hundreds of years removed from the life which had once animated Poundbury and made it a scene of activity. Fires must once have burned in the camp, women in skins cooked and men worked their flints and bare children run tumbling and playing across the grass. Some of them lay buried deeply beneath the smooth turf, uncaring that a few yards from them and vibrating their dry bones every hour or so ran engines along the railway tunnel which pierces one side of the huge mound. Someday our civilisation will be a memory and a ruin and a new race of man will disturb our bones in their resting place as they tunnel and bore. The graves of the dead without name can be ravished without sacrilege. Close to Poundbury, down the valley towards the town, runs a line of pylons, slender and beautiful in their long-reaching perspectives. One day their rusted frames will be dug from the alluvium of the Frome and puzzle wiseheads as Poundbury puzzles wiseheads today.

'There was some sense in building a camp up here,' said my friend. 'It must have been easy to see your enemies coming, and when there were no enemies in sight what better thing to do than admire the view. Perhaps they built it here for the view more than for protection against the enemies they had. We don't credit these ancient peoples with enough artistic sense.'

'Well, all you need to do today is admire the view. You needn't bother about enemies.'

'No? Others are bothering though.' He nodded towards the rifle range and I saw small brown figures stretched out on the grass and heard the thin crack of rifle shots.

'Today we are more civilised. Only some of us keep an eye on enemies, while others admire the view. In the old days you had to do both things yourself.'

As a rule I do not like museums. There is always far too much to see and not enough time. If you make up your mind to go and look at one section, say the natural history section, you are constantly aware of the temptation to wander away and look at the ceramics or the geological exhibits. It is hard to disabuse the mind of its conception that the first duty towards a museum is to see everything in it, and the gentle race from case to case and from hall to hall is, in itself, an exhibition of man's pitiable febrility of mind.

I wanted to avoid Dorchester's museum. My friend would not allow this.

'If a town goes to the trouble of collecting antiquities from the neighbourhood, and a curator spends no little amount of time, generally for a negligible salary, arranging and cataloguing exhibits, the least one can do is to go and look at them. Besides, who knows what may not be learned in a museum. I once got a very good recipe for an excellent cheese pudding from a man I met in the British Museum.'

'I don't mind visiting the museums, if they are as you say. From my experience most of them never rise any higher than a few collections of flint arrowheads, some doubtful pieces of terracotta pottery, and cases of foreign birds brought back from his world tour by the local squire.'

I was taken to the museum, and I am glad now that I went. Dorchester's museum is quite different from any other. It is small enough to prevent a man from surfeiting himself with the exhibits, it is well arranged, and has less unlabelled exhibits than any other museum of its size that I know. Most important, its exhibits are interesting and nearly all concerned with Dorset and Dorchester. If you buy the official guide you can, with a little patience and a great deal of satisfaction, see illustrated, from the cases of exhibits, the story of mankind in Dorset (and therefore in England) through the ages. If you do not care to trace the history of man through the Neolithic, the various Bronze and Iron Ages up to the coming of the Romans, then you can go and stand on the tessellated pavements, found from time to time in Dorchester, which are laid in the main hall, or stare at the collection of man-traps and try to decide of which one it was that Thomas Hardy wrote: 'It produced, when set, a vivid impression that it was endowed with life and exhibited the combined aspects of a stork, a crocodile and a scorpion.' A queer beast.

Nowhere did I see any of the useless abracadabra which is often turned out of the large houses of the county and, for want of a better home, presented to the museum, and I would have spent more time in there if I had been allowed to by my friend. With true tourist energy he professed to have sucked the marrow from the museum bone within half an hour and was impatient to be off.

'I have had enough of the past. Let us go out into the present again,' he protested. So we did. But the past still clung to us, for we found ourselves having tea in a building which had served as the lodgings of the hated Judge Jeffries. Today, where the infamous judge bullied serving wenches and thundered at frightened men, there are no sounds more alarming than the rattle of teacups, the polite, subdued chatter of tourists and the innocuous music of a gramophone. He held his Bloody Assize in a room at the Antelope Hotel around the corner from the teahouse. I wonder if the people of Dorset flocked to the hanging fairs then to see the last moments of men and women they loved.

Judge Jefferies was not the first to bring mass tragedy into the lives of the Dorchester people. An older, more terrible enemy than any man visited them more than once. Three or four times the town was fired and burnt to the ground almost, and I think these fires explain Dorchester's anomalous architecture features. In a county whose most characteristic buildings are the colour-washed thatched cottages, it is strange to find that there are very few such cottages or thatched houses in Dorchester itself. Except for one or two buildings there are few old houses in Dorchester. Thatch was good fuel for fire, and the primitive firefighting implements must have made poor show against the blaze that burst from roof to roof. A contemporary writer describes Dorchester after one of these fires as 'a ruinated Troy or decayed Carthage.'

Some of the old hooks used for tearing the thatch off the cottages, and the primitive water pumps are in the museum. Men were quicker in inventing the means to fight one another than they were in fashioning weapons to combat fire.

After tea we walked about the town, forgetting the guidebook and content to wander. We found ourselves lazing by the river with a flotilla of ducks rivalling the roar of a tiny weir with their quacking. Trees came low over the water and, across the valley plain, cattle stood silently in the meadows like dark shadows against the wall of the sky. We followed the shaded walks that mark the site of the old walls that once fortified the town and suddenly we were standing before the bronze figure of a seated, bare-headed man, staring into the gathering mist of the twilight. We stood for a while, remembering the man who brought so much fame to the town and the county which he called Casterbridge and Wessex. His love for the county was no flamboyant, boisterous affection. It flowed in a deep spirit, steady as the hills of Wessex and as pure as the air and water that move across the country. The quiet streets of the town, the hedge-sides laced with a border of flowering cow parsley, the long downs broken by patches of gorse and the rudely-cut figures from a past age, the copses in the hollows of the hills and the small clouds of sheep along the ridges all bring back memories of his works. Dorset belongs to Hardy as surely as Exmoor is Blackmore's and Cumberland Walpole's. His statue stands, a silent symbol of a respect which will endure for generations. The tragic Tess and the pathetic Jude are not the only phantoms that live again in the blue evening mist of the Dorset evenings, and Dorset was in need of no statue to keep the memory green of her poet and lover.

We went down the main street into the life of the town. There were lights now in the shop windows, there was movement, the quick happy movement of the end of the working day, on the pavements. A notice in a grocer's shop caught our eyes and we stopped and looked at one another and the same thought passed between us.

Maybe you are not fond of cheese, and recognise it only as something that comes tagging along at the end of a meal to be toyed with while you exercise your teeth on biscuits. Do Camembert, Gruyere, Gorgonzola, Cheddar, Cheshire, mean nothing to you; is there no poetry, no music in the sweet roll of their names for you? Have you never thought that a meal would never pass through its tedious courses to leave you alone with the cheese? Then what follows cannot interest you.

Dorset Blue Vinny Cheese – the notice said, and we had never tasted it. We decided to repair the deficiency in our cheese education, and entered the shop.

Dorset Blue is not a cream cheese. It is made from the skimmed milk, and the curds do not press so well as the curds of richer cheeses made from unskimmed milk, so that the 'vinny' soon attacks the interstices of the cheese, giving it its characteristic blue marbling. Sometimes the blue marking failed to appear and the only remedy, at least in those days when every cottage and farm had its own beer barrel, was to wrap it in a cloth and hang it under the bung to catch the drippings. This invariably improved the taste and brought on the marking.

The shop man did not want to sell us any cheese.

'You'm come at the wrong time of the year,' he said. 'It's made during the summer and it's nearly all gone by the end of the autumn. It doan't keep long and the piece I've got is hardly vit to be put on the table. I should have had that notice out of the window but we've been so busy, and I forgot it was there.'

He could not persuade us from our cheese. Good or indifferent, we wanted it and we had it. It was obvious that it had lost its first glory.

'You know why they call it "vinny"?' asked the shopman as he wrapped it up.

'No,' I said as I took it from him.

'It's because of the markings. They're like blue veins and vinny is the Dorset way of saying veiny.'

We walked out of the shop and my companion turned to me.

'Did you believe that?'

'About the veins?'

'Yes.'

'Why not, it sounds a very likely reason.'

'Not at all. Vinny means no such thing as you would know if you had ever made a study of philology. Philology is not a matter of guesswork, it is an exact science. Finew is the Anglo-Saxon for 'to become' or 'make mouldy'. From finew we get finewed, meaning mouldy. Now no philologist will dispute that the West of England dialect has a trick of substituting v's for f's, so we get vinnewed and finally vinney, and the name of the cheese comes from its blue mould, and not from the veins.'

'How do you know all this? You're not a philologist.'

'I know, but I like cheese, and before we decided to come to Dorchester I guessed we might be getting some Blue Vinny so I did, or rather, had done for me, a little research work. You can't appreciate a good cheese only by the taste, you must know all about its name and how it's made. You knew how it was made, but I knew about its name. Now let's go back to the hotel and see about its taste.'

If you want to know what Blue Vinny Cheese tastes like go to Dorset and get some.

CHAPTER 18

BIDEFORD

When'er I tread old By-the-Ford
I conjure up the thought
'Twas here a Grenville trod
And here a Raleigh wrought.

This is better poetry than one would expect from a postman, and if it has a little breathlessness then it shows how truly the postman who wrote it has worked his own personality into the lines. So sang Edward Capern, a remarkable man of the nineteenth century, and a very good postman, who was known as the Devonshire Burns. Capern was a Tiverton man, but he was Bideford's postman for many years, and Bideford has decided to adopt him.

That his thoughts as he climbed the Bideford streets and hills were often of Grenville and Raleigh, I do not dispute, yet if I had to do much walking up and down the hills my thoughts would soon pass from matters historical. If you live in Bideford long, I suppose, you get used to the hills and Capern probably took them in his stride.

I like Bideford. I liked it the moment I stepped from the train on to the railway platform, for the platform is one of the best introductions to Bideford. The station stands on a slight elevation on the east side of the river Torridge, which comes rolling down from Dartmoor to meet its sister, the Taw, below Appledore, there to join hands and venture out across the Bar to find the long Atlantic surges. Across the Torridge runs Bideford bridge, the main approach to the town, and rising up the steep bank that fronts the river is Bideford, row after row of houses, dotted with inns, shops and churches, and atop the hill stand clumps of dark elms making distant silhouettes against the sky. Kingsley called it 'the little white town of Bideford.' In places the cream-washed walls of the houses try to live up to his description, but mostly the buildings are grey and red-bricked, a pleasing jumble of colours.

Bideford reminded me of the plump, busy women who sit in its own market minding their baskets of eggs and bowls of rich cream. It is just like a countrywoman, kindly, but ready to take affront at the slightest sign of condescension, healthy, and proud of nothing so much as its children. And Bideford has a lot of children to clack about, not all of them good, some of them a little mad and one or two no more than dream figures. It takes time to decide which were real and which only fiction. Charles Kingsley, whose statue stands at the end of the quay, has so peopled the town with characters from *Westward Ho!* that nowadays it is difficult, I found, not to imagine that once Salvation Yeo did stand on the quayside showing his wonderful horn and telling his fantastic tales of sea adventure to a crowd of gaping yokels and seamen, while the young Amyas Leigh listened, wide-eyed, from the fringe of the crowd. And poor Rose Salterne, the victim of the stupidity which seems to be accounted a virtue in the heroines of romances, was she never more than fiction and never did actually live in Bridgeland Street?

If Rose did not exist, it was in Bridgeland Street that one of Bideford's mad children lived and died. He was Thomas Stucley, the son of Oliver Cromwell's chaplain, whose brain was turned with overstudy and of whom it was said that 'When the Duke of Marlborough laid siege to any town in Flanders, Mr Stucley would draw a plan of the place upon his kitchen floor, which, according to the Devonshire custom, was made of lime and ashes; and by the intelligence of the newspapers he would work at the plan with a pickaxe, so that every conquest cost him a new floor.' Still, Mr Stucley and no doubt the Duke of Marlborough, too, had he known, would regard the cost of a new floor as a small price to pay for the glory of a victory.

I walked from the station across the bridge to the town. Bideford, the town by the ford, is now the town by the bridge. Today the bridge is a wide, well-paved thoroughfare, lighted by gas lamps that at night cast little flares of light upon the dark waters of the tide that flows between the irregularly spaced arches. The arches are of different spans because, so it is said, when the original structure was thrown across the river in the fourteenth century, some spans were endowed by rich folk and some by the poor, and the bigger the span the richer the endowment. The truth, I feel, is likely to be that the placing of the spans was dictated by the formation of the bed of the river and the need to build on solid rock.

It was hard to imagine as I watched the stream of cars and omnibuses going over the bridge, that at one time it had been so narrow that pedestrians had been forced to step back into little recesses placed over each pillar to make way for the strings of pack-horses with their swaying panniers full of merchandise, for the bridge was an important link in the great pack-road that came up from Cornwall, through Devon and Somerset towards London. The maintenance of the bridge was of supreme importance and the bridge trustees grew to be the wealthiest body in Bideford, and they did not confine their activities to looking after the bridge. They endowed charities, scholarships, and laid down the finest cellar of wines in all Devon to grace the board at the famous Bridge dinners.

The dinners and the cellar have gone now, and with them a great deal of Bideford's commercial importance. As a port Bideford once ranked as the third in the kingdom; now its glory lies in the past, a distinction it shares with towns of more modern birth.

To anyone who enjoys smoking, Bideford should have an affectionate appeal, for it was in one of its warehouses that the first consignment of tobacco to England lay. I wonder that some enterprising manufacturer of tobacco has not had the sound commercial instinct to take advantage of the advertising possibilities of this fact and name a brand of tobacco after Bideford. As I walked up to my hotel I occupied myself with inventing the name of the brand. The best I could manage was Bideford Bridge Brand, with Bideford Mixture, and the slogan – *The Tobacco that kept Raleigh Cool* – as a runner-up. Through dinner I was working on the wrapper. It was to be simple and effective, a picture of Bideford quay with the town and bridge in a fading perspective, while the heroic figure of Raleigh, in slashed doublet, a sword cocked from his side, smoking a long clay pipe, should stand in the foreground surrounded by a crowd of wondering little boys. So engrossed was I with my scheme that I scarcely noticed that I was being served with the usual unimaginative dinner in which English hotels excel.

The next morning, on my way to the parish church, I called in at a tobacconists for some tobacco and before I could check myself had said:

'Two ounces of the Bideford Bridge Brand, please.'

The shopman looked at me enquiringly.

'Bideford—'

'The Tobacco that kept Raleigh Cool,' I said, wondering at his stupidity, and then recoiling at my own.

'Don't keep that kind, sir.'

I asked for my usual make and fled from the shop.

The parish church is full of the memories of the Grenville family. There seems to be a certain amount of controversy as to the correct spelling of the name. The greatest of the Grenvilles was Sir Richard, a Bideford man, and it was from the town that he went to die, as every schoolboy knows, near 'Flores in the Azores.' The story of the *Revenge* is as moving as anything in Homer. I found the brass in the church which had been erected by a descendant to commemorate Sir Richard's death. Few people could read the last words of that courtly Elizabethan seaman and not respond to their noble simplicity.

'Here die I, Richard Grenville, with a joyful and quiet mind...'

How many of us, when the time comes, will be ready to go with a joyful and quiet mind? They were a rough crew, the Elizabethan seamen, barbarous at times, but there is no disputing their valour and dignity in the face of death. They were used to danger, they had faced death close enough more than once while their ships tossed in the great troughs of the ocean; they had stood with only cold steel and the strength of their sails and ropes between them and oblivion too many times to shirk the final combat when it came. They were seldom careless of their lives, yet they never let the fear of death stand between them and what they considered their duty. It is easy to call them pirates, ruffians. They were also men of principle. They lived in an age when force was the wisest law, and if they fought with a wild joy, at least they fought to gain possession of new lands, not from some obscure quarrel of politicians.

For a long time most of the trade with the Americas, Holland, France and Spain came up the silver estuary of the Torridge. It was during the eighteenth century that Bideford's trade declined, slowly losing its importance because of the deprivations of the privateers who harried the shipping in Bideford's Golden Bay, making their headquarters on Lundy Island. The oak screen of the tower in the church is proof of this trade. It is made from the ends of old pews and benches from the church, and the carvings which decorated the seats of the wealthy merchants of the time symbolise the sea and the distant lands that brought them wealth.

I stood before it looking at the carvings. There were grotesque dolphins, sea serpents, feathered Indians, seamen hauling on ropes, strange fruit, flying fish and here and there the arms of the Grenville family. While I was standing there, the church caretaker, who had been polishing the pews, came up to me and asked me if I would like to see the fine silver chalice and communion tankard which had been with the church since the seventeenth century. He took me into the vestry and let me see them. His face was as red and round as a pippin and it shone with pleasure as he saw me admiring the silver work.

'Here's something else that might interest 'ee, zur.' He pulled from a cupboard an old church register and showed me the actual entries, in the curious Elizabethan script, of the baptism in 1588 and the death, a year later, of one Rawley, a Winganditoian. This Rawley (the spelling of Raleigh has even more variations than Grenville) was a North American Indian, brought back to England by Sir Richard Grenville as his servant. He must have caused a stir among the women of the town, though the men were probably used to his kind from their voyages. Rawley did not survive long in the boisterous climate of Devon.

'Poor li'l chap,' said the caretaker. "E didn't last long. Reckon he must have died of homesickness.'

I wonder whether it was homesickness or the climate.

I walked about the streets after I left the church and I noticed that in almost every shop which sold foodstuffs there were large bowls of what looked like cooked spinach, of a black and shiny texture. My curiosity got the better of me and I went into a shop and enquired what the stuff was.

'Laver,' came the answer.

Laver, I was told, is a species of seaweed which is collected locally and is fried or made into cakes. In Bideford it has some popularity, but I cannot say that it looked appetising to me. I was asked to try some. I refused with haste and afterwards regretted my cowardice, until I read in a guidebook that it is a food 'which some people profess to like.' I fancied there was an ominous intent in that phrase and congratulated myself upon my conservatism.

The train that took me away from Bideford passed along the river towards Barnstaple (a town which, while you are in Bideford, it is not wise to praise, for there is a great rivalry between the two). It was a sad stretch of river. The gallant ships of the seafaring Elizabethans have gone, their timbers mouldered into dust, or overgrown with seaweed on hidden reefs, and now the great ships which bore England's cargoes about the seas before and during the last war are coming home to these quiet estuaries and rivers to end their days, quietly rusting, their decks alive only with the cry of seabirds and the flap of washing hung out by caretakers who inhabit the great corpses like beetles. It was a sad sight, the ships which are wanted no more because there are not enough cargoes to fill their holds, come back to Bideford, the home of so much of England's shipping wealth and commercial greatness, to finish their days by the river down which once swept the vessels of Grenville to find the far Americas and spread the glory of the Virgin Queen across every ocean.

CHAPTER 19

SOMEWHERE IN CORNWALL

On the Cornish coast, somewhere between Fowey and Falmouth, there is a certain fishing village. It is not well known. It has attracted no colony of artists to disturb the rightful atmosphere of the village inn, nor does it have many visitors during the summer. I am not going to give its name, for that would undoubtedly incense the few *foreigners*, as the village folk term those who spend their holidays there, who treasure its secret. Besides, it would detract from its pleasure to make it easy to find. The joys which are hard to come by are the sweetest.

On the other hand, I do not wish to be accused of being a curmudgeon, selfish in my pleasure, so I will give enough clues to enable the diligent seeker to identify the village.

If you are looking for the ideal fishing village where you can spend your summer holiday, forgetting your worries by bathing in tiny coves with only the gulls and the cliffs for company, and by wandering along brackened headlands where thyme and gorse fill the air with their scent, then this is the village for you.

There are scores of villages in Cornwall which are just as pleasant and in looking for this one you may discover the charm of a dozen other places, for the Cornish coast is lavish in its beauty and its villages have a character which no other coastal villages in England can rival; which is a pathetic admission from a Devon man, but nevertheless the truth.

I have spent several holidays in this village, during the high summer, when the days were drowsy with heat and there was always the pleasing rattle of mowing-machines filling the scented air. It was lovely then. How much lovelier, I used to think, would it be in the spring. I always longed to see it in the spring and at last my desire drew me there when I had no excuse for going, and every reason for remaining where I was, which was far enough from Cornwall to make the thought of the village a tantalising prospect of joy.

The village lies at the narrow mouth of a short, steep valley. A tiny freshet runs through the valley, hardly enough to fill a duck pond and almost hidden by a waving mass of garlic-mustard and tall cow parsley.

It was raining as I walked down the steep, high-hedged lane that leads from the top of the hill to the narrow-mouthed cove around which are grouped the grey-slated houses and cottages of the villagers. I did not mind the rain. It was a gentle, caressing drizzle that soaked into the eager ground and filled the runnels at the lane's side with a brown-tinged torrent that sang over the worn outcrops of slate. Hart's tongue ferns dripped water on me from the high banks, and from a farm gate a sheepdog puppy came out and sniffed at my legs. A jackdaw balancing on top of a telegraph pole muttered something rude as I passed and, feeling happy, I returned the compliment. The jackdaw flew away, disgusted.

There were violets still in the bankside, not easily seen against the flaring pads of primroses. I came to the first houses and saw fuchsias blooming in pots behind the windows, and I wondered how long it would be before they were blooming in the hedges of the gardens which were now full of spring colours. A wave of heavy scent made me aware of a clump of wallflowers rooted in the sparse soil between the roof slates of a shed, their crimson heads held stiffly against the gentle wind.

I turned a corner and immediately the roar and call of the sea was all around me. The wind was suddenly stronger, full of salt. It drummed against my face, and my ears were filled with the clamour of gulls circling over the tiny harbour. Nothing had changed since my last visit. Grey and white cottages lined the roadway and crab nets were stretched over the wall which separated the road from the beach. High on the other side of the cove stood the white clump of coastguard buildings and the slender flagpole from which I have never seen a flag flown. Beyond the blunt nose of the headland which projected halfway across the harbour mouth the open sea tossed and heaved under the low pall of a rainy sky.

I passed by the general store, its window crammed to bursting point with an indiscrimination of wares arranged in a way which would have given a professional window-dresser apoplexy. A line of washing straggled up the far cliff slope with, I fancy, the same blue shirt and pants that used to grace it during the summer of my last visit. I could have sworn to the shirt. The pants I was doubtful about.

The first persons I saw were three men mending lobster pots in a fishing store at the head of the beach. The door was open and they were laughing at some joke, while ten yards away the full tide spouted over the rocks, tossing its fringe of bladder wrack and refuse. They were bareheaded, dark haired, and dressed in blue jerseys. They nodded to me politely and then went on with their work, joking as though I were not still leaning against the doorpost watching them.

If I had started a conversation they would have replied and been affable. By themselves they were diffident of strangers and never eager, more from shyness than want of matters to talk about, to take the lead in a conversation. The noise of a heavy breakwater growling over loose shingle made me look up. They made no movement, but I knew that they had heard the sea. Never did they forget the sea. It had become part of their lives so that even now, as they plied hazel boughs into the plinth of their lobster pots, they knew which rocks the tide had still to cover, and how the wind and currents were setting. The changing face of the sky and the quick lift and fall of the soft Cornish mist and rain were things which had been with them since birth and which they had come to know with a precision that was now more an instinct than conscious knowledge.

I went down on to the beach, past the little white post office. The only concessions to the conventional furnishings of a seaside resort were a weighing machine standing against the side of the building used as a sort of club for the fishermen, and the display of postcards in the post office window. The weighing machine, filmed with a dew of rain, was crowned by a villainous looking herring gull which stared at me with its lustreless yellow eyes and then launched itself into the air to join its fellows crying along the cliffs. It was a handsome, cold-minded bird, graceful in the air, revelling in its powers of flight, and like all its kind, a most rapacious thief, ready to steal from or murder any living thing too weak to resist its ugly curved beak.

Drawn up on the beach, out of reach of the tide, were the motor boats used in the lobster and crab fishing which provides the men of the village with a living. The motors and screws of some boats were carefully covered. On the bottom boards of one or two were broken pieces of starfish and the white fans of coral brought up in the pots, and in a heap on the beach were some spider-crabs, useless, grotesque, like fantastic spiders from the cave of some lurid story for boys. F.H. 9, F.H. 14… all the boats had registration numbers and some bore names, painted in unsteady characters, across the bows and gunwales.

I ate my bread and cheese lunch with the landlord of the Ship Inn for company. He is a tall, boyish-faced man, with a happy habit of finishing his remarks, whether humorous or not, with a gurgling laugh. He takes life merrily and I found it disconcerting for a while to hear him chuckling as he told me, with a wealth of detail conned from his morning paper, how an American gangster was at that moment being executed in Chicago.

'Ay, they have a proper game with 'em over there. Shaive off their hair, all of it, they do, and then sit 'em in the 'lectric chair. By Gor, tes some game, I tell 'ee.'

'It's quicker than being hanged,' I said.

'I don't knaw 'bout that. Tes more unnatural though, to be 'lectrocuted.' He gurgled happily and began to set up the pins of the skittle-table. Games in public houses differ from county to county. In Kent there are always darts and in Cumberland dominoes. In this village the fishermen prefer table-skittles with their beer.

The bar was dark from the shadow of the headland that protects the village from the channel gales. Just inside the door was a coloured plate of a blue-chequered racing pigeon and on the other walls two realistic engravings entitled 'Horses in a Storm' and 'Groom and Horse.' There was, I thought, little need for this last title, for although the picture was bad there was not the slightest chance of anyone mixing up the horse with the groom or the groom with the horse. I only had to count their legs to be sure which was which.

The landlord shook his head and pursed his lips as I asked him about the winter.

'Purty bad, it's been. There's been a tidy few gales and the boats hav'n been out more 'n a score of times since September. Ess, tes been tidy bad for some of the men.'

He was not exaggerating. Gales keep the boats locked in the harbour and while they idle there the pots are swept away from their moorings and lost. Only men of stubborn spirit could face such setbacks with fortitude. The men grumble but never despair, otherwise they could not wrest a living from the capricious sea.

In a glass case on the counter were rows of little figures of pirates, jockeys and Long John Silvers. They were ingenious figures modelled in clay about the wishbones of chickens, the prongs of the wishbone forming the legs. The pirates with cocked hats and black patches stood in a bow-legged array above the brightly painted jockeys, and above them all stood a massive Long John Silver, made from the bone of a turkey, brass earrings, crooked smile, but no parrot. The landlord saw me looking at them and said:

'There's more money in that kind of thing these days, than in fishing. Feller in the village makes 'em up and sells 'em. He does quite well.'

When I left him, I walked up the hill on the other side of the village and out to the sweep of cliff that runs back from the headland which protects the village. Here, beneath crimson-trunked firs and pines, over the short turf and dead bracken, was waving the gold of wild daffodils, a long, seething, billowing sheet of colour. On the rocks below, the sea broke in white foam and gulls went to and fro along the shore, crying, and beating the wind with their wings. Long streamers of soft rain swept across the sea, and as I watched there came through the mist the steady beat of a motor and slowly around the headland a dark shape moved across the tossing water and gradually disappeared into the murk. On board were three men, perhaps the three men I had seen in the store laughing. They were probably still laughing, though that would not make them careless of the work in hand. There were pots to be lifted, lobsters to be caught and sold, fresh bait to be set and nets to be shot... there was always something to be done, and in the end a man sitting in his room, fiddling with clay and wishbones, made a better living than they did with no part of their hardships...

I walked back through the village, wondering if the day of physical courage was gone. Strength was no longer capable of earning a living for itself. These inshore fishermen were antiquated, working hard and making little, and helpless against the competition which came from an industry organised by men of brain and worked by giant trawlers and the latest scientific apparatus. They would have to go, already their sons were leaving the sea to become mechanics and clerks, to get themselves jobs which involved no great dangers and brought them food and the comfort of contented minds. In some villages the change is nearly complete, fishermen have become landlords and their wives landladies, and their living is made during the summer by catering for visitors. Soon all the Cornish villages will be seeking to catch the visitor and make his fortnight by the sea feed them during the winter. But this village, I think, will be the last to make the change. Even now the summer brings a little more money, easier money, but fishing is in their blood. They never regard it in any heroic light. It is a job which they know how to do, and do. At the moment they want no other life. Why should they worry about the years ahead?

crimson cats
audio books

Everyman's England
Victor Canning
Abridged by Michael Bartlett and read by Charles Collingwood

Everyman's England

Victor Canning

Crimson Cats Audio Books

ISBN: 978 0 95513 943 7

Running time: 79 minutes

The audio book of *Everyman's England*, read by Charles Collingwood (perhaps better known as Brian Aldridge in *The Archers*), brings the story of Victor Canning's travels around England to life. In her review of the audio book in *The Times*, Christina Hardyment wrote 'after listening to Charles Collingwood... voicing these pin-sharp evocations of England in the 1930s I predict that Canning will soon be rediscovered. He describes the fiddly arrangements of a sleeper compartment in a way that makes listening impossible without frequent chuckles, and he sees into the heart of things'.

This recording is published by Crimson Cats Audio Books and features eleven of the places that Victor Canning visited. It is available as a CD for £10.99 plus p&p or as an MP3 download for £6.98; both are available from the website www.crimsoncats.co.uk. To order the CD by post please contact Crimson Cats on 01379 854888.

Have you enjoyed this book?

If so, why not write a review on your favourite website?

Thanks very much for buying this Summersdale book.

www.summersdale.com